Night of the Klan, A Reporter's Story

By

Robert M. Reed

© 2002 by Robert M. Reed. All rights reserved.

No part of this book may be reproduced, stored in a retrieval system, or transmitted by any means, electronic, mechanical, photocopying, recording, or otherwise, without written permission from the author.

ISBN: 0-7596-9927-5 (Ebook)
ISBN: 0-7596-9928-3 (Softcover)
ISBN: 0-7596-9929-1 (Dustjacket)

This book is printed on acid free paper.

1stBooks – rev. 6/11/02

TABLE OF CONTENTS

Acknowledgements v
Introduction vii
Prologue ix
The Day Before (Klan History) 1
    The 19th Century Klan 1
    The New Century 6
    The Middle Years 14
    The War Years 1940s 19
Morning (Chapter 1) 25
Early Afternoon (Chapter 2) 29
Late Afternoon (Chapter 3) 39
Evening (Chapter 4) 57
Nightfall (Chapter 5) 66
Midnight (Chapter 6) 72
Daybreak (Chapter 7) 78
High Noon (Chapter 8) 83
Another Day (Chapter 9) 92
Another Night (Chapter 10) 100
Epilogue (1970s and beyond) 109
Bibliography 113
Index 117
About The Author 121

ACKNOWLEDGEMENTS

Probably the most essential part of my research, aside from my own personal file of notes and written records were, the investigative records of then Johnson County (Indiana) prosecutor Joe VanValer. The prosecutor's files, more than 250 pages in length, documents the sworn testimony of numerous Klan members as well as Klan followers. The files also included much of the criminal casework conducted by the Indiana State Police. In additional there were newspaper accounts, some brief and some lengthy, in more than a dozen newspapers over the period of 1967 through 1972. The exact reports of both Associated Press and United Press International were also preserved and retained in preparing this book. Additional investigative information, and a staggering assortment of more than 2,000 documents were eventually provided by the U.S. Department of Justice and The Federal Bureau of Investigation.

Here let me also express my very deepest personal appreciation to Indiana State Police detective Richard Bumps, and law enforcement officers at all levels that not only provided information to me in the aftermath, but unflinchingly protected my family and my self during the darkest days of this story. I will be forever grateful to them all.

INTRODUCTION

In a sense there are two books here.

The first is a very candid 100-year history of one of this nation's most legendary hate groups, The Ku Klux Klan. The second is a reporter's personal account of how the KKK operated during the 1960s. Much of it, the elaborate organization of the Klan of the 60s and role of those who opposed it, has never before been revealed in its full context.

My son, among others, says the history is necessary to allow the reader to understand how the Klan was nearly extinguished time and again only to ignite years later. Organized hate has always been that way.

To those seeking to cut to the chase of the Klan during the 1960s, plunge forward to the personal account.

During the 1960s the Klan had perhaps its greatest impact on American history in general and the Civil Rights Movement in general. As a journalist in the Midwest it provided the most fascinating and at times the most terrifying days of my life. During that time I had access to the secret meetings, witnessed their ceremonies, learned their passwords, and followed their campaigns to establish themselves once again in the hearts of the misguided.

It was a time when I met personally with their Exalted Clylops, Kleagles, Grand Dragons and Imperial Wizards. Ultimately that journalistic journey turned dangerous. I was held at gunpoint by Klan guards, threatened with death by late night telephone calls, barricaded in my home with my family, and persuaded to testify before a Grand Jury.

In the course of the decade I was able to accumulate lengthy notes, newspaper accounts, wire service teletypes, and personal interviews. In the years that followed a great deal of documenting information was made available through the United States Justice Department, The Freedom of Information Act, and the cooperation of other law enforcement agencies.

The entire story is presented here, in The Night of the Klan, A Reporter's Story.

PROLOGUE

Early in 1967 the 'new' Ku Klux Klan appeared on the verge of making inroads into the Midwestern United States.

With a Southern-based membership in excess of 40,000 the so-called Invisible Empire was now anxious to spread its message northward and perhaps once again rekindle the glory days of the 1920s when millions were on the membership rolls and regularly donned white robes to burn crosses in dark nights across America.

Imperial Wizard Robert Shelton, who headed what was clearly the most powerful of the Klan groups of the 1960s, the Knights of the Klu Klux Klan, was personally carrying his recruitment programs into states like Michigan, Ohio, and Indiana during the early months of 1967. Shelton had made earlier trips, and some were showing signs of success, Certainly the Imperial Wizard's efforts had attracted the attention of the Federal Bureau of Investigation.

In March of 1967 Shelton again headed into the Midwest and so did the mechanism of the F.B.I. On March 15, 1967 the Washington D.C. headquarters of the FBI sent highly confidential messages to a number of offices alerting them to the Imperial Wizard's travels and suggesting the possible use of informants to monitor Shelton's activities. Names of a few likely informants were also mentioned. Copies of that particular memorandum that day went to FBI offices in Birmingham, Charlotte and Indianapolis.

It concluded:

"Indianapolis is holding in abeyance dissemination of this information to local U.S. Secret Service and military intelligence agencies pending bureau approval."

The FBI wanted their Klan surveillance kept secret even to the point of screening out other federal agencies and not even informing certain military installations that some storehouses of weapons and explosives may be targets of Klan-related thefts.

Specifically Shelton movements were part of the FBI's well-concealed counter-intelligence operation known as COINTELPRO. It had been quietly launched in September of 1964 specifically to "expose, disrupt and other wise neutralize the activities of various Klans and hate organizations, their leadership and adherents."

The secret directive further noted:

"The Bureau considers it vital that we expose the identities and activities of such groups and where possible disrupt their efforts. No counter-intelligence action may be initiated by the field without specific Bureau authorization. You are cautioned that the new endeavor is such that under no circumstances should the existence of the program be made known outside the Bureau and appropriate within-office security should be afforded this sensitive operation."

Now COINTELPRO was being called into play in the Indianapolis region. On that very same day the Indianapolis office of the FBI received a second secret memorandum from Washington. It directed the local office to proceed to contact a special list of informants and "all sources whose identities are concealed... (And have)...furnished reliable information in the past."

The war had begun.

Over 100 years of Ku Klux Klan history was attempting to repeat itself once again.

Night of the Klan, A Reporter's Story

THE DAY BEFORE

The 19th Century Klan

The secret session was held somewhere within the village of Pulaski in Giles County, Tennessee. Some accounts suggest it was not a single meeting but a series of meetings in December of 1865 that led to the formation of the Ku Klux Klan.

Only months later the great Civil War had ended leaving many southern whites bitter from their overwhelming loss and fearful of the economic result. Six men, all of them former Confederate soldiers, formed the initial group.

While few documents survived the organization's initial formation, it was clear that the group was small. Around the table of a small law office was John B. Kennedy, James. R. Crow, Frank O. McCord, Richard Reed, Calvin Jones, and John C. Lester. There may have been others, but not many.

There was a discussion about the naming of the organization. At first there were plans to operate under the identity of the Knights of the Circle, but some felt the name would be then be confused the previously existing Knights of the Golden Circle. Eventually it was suggested that the group be known as the Knights of Kuklos, since kuklos was the Greek word for circle. Further discussion came up with the Kuklos Klan, and ultimately the group settled upon the Ku Klux Klan.

At what some suggest was a second meeting of the Klan, that same December in the ruins of a house damaged by a storm on the day after Christmas of 1865, the group declared itself the first Den of the Ku Klux Klan.

For all of its seeming secrecy, other Dens of the Klan were rapidly added throughout the South. The rituals and ceremonies of the group seemed to appeal to many, and the thinly disguised threat of revenge and retribution was appealing to even more. Some accounts suggest the group's use of white sheets as costumes were to invoke the memory of Confederate soldiers who had died in battle not so long ago. It too was appealing in the South. The Congressional elections of 1866 proved a further boon for the growing Klan organization in the South. The Klan seemed to offer resistance, legal or otherwise, against the so-called Radical Republicans and the federal government's efforts to establish new political and economic status for blacks.

By early 1867 the federal government moved to put into force a series of Reconstruction Acts that served to abolish existing Confederate state governments and instead establish military districts. Essentially the Congressional-like districts were created to allow previously excluded black citizens the opportunity to take part in elections. Conflict and turmoil ensured throughout the South, driving vast numbers of white men into the ranks of the Ku Klux Klan. Klan Dens were taking form throughout Tennessee, Alabama, Georgia, Mississippi and other areas. By the spring of 1867 it was determined that the various Klan groups would send delegates to a single assembly in Nashville, Tennessee. At a secret location, possibly the Maxwell House, a series of sessions were held to formalize ceremonies and rituals, to draft a "prescript of the Order," and to make plans to oppose in every way possible the enactment of the federal Reconstruction Acts. Nominated and elected by acclamation as Imperial Wizard at the meeting of Klans was a popular Confederate veteran, Nathan Bedford Forrest. Forrest had held the rank of lieutenant general of the Confederate States of America and had remained popular with former soldiers and the civilian population. The group also decreed that the full organization of Klans would now be known as the Invisible Empire.

As the newly chosen Imperial Wizard, Forrest unfurled a rather ambitious and elaborate organization of the membership. The Invisible Empire, the Wizard instructed, would reach to the thirteen states of the original Confederacy, and also to Maryland. To further the group's growth the Wizard would appoint a Grand Dragon for each of the Empire's Realms that amounted to more or less one for each state. In turn each Grand Dragon would appoint a Grand Titan for each district of the Realm, an area roughly in comparison to a Congressional district. Next each Grand Titan would appoint a group of six Furies for Provinces of the Titan's Dominion. The Provinces would generally correspond in area to a state's particular counties. Also detailed were the appointment of even more extensive branches Klan units that called for a Grand Giant, Goblins, Cyclops, and finally Night-Hawks. Broken down in quasi-military units each group would be headed by staff officers with such titles as Magi, Monk, Turk and Sentinel. Given the highest rank in units were those "known and designated as Ghouls."

While organization chart and other details that were a part of the overall "prescript of the Order" were to remain secret, a few copies were said to have survived after being taken from the Nashville meeting to a printer back in the community Pulaski. The few copies survived even after all documents were specifically ordered destroyed by Klan officials some years later.

In the weeks and months that followed the initial meeting in Nashville the Klan continued to organize and evolve. There were reports of Klan activity in a number of surrounding states. Several newspaper stories in July of 1867 reported Klan members taking part in July Fourth celebrations which often consisted of hooded riders aboard sheeted horses. There were also newspaper accounts of less public activities being linked to the nightriders of the Klan. Even in the early stages of operation the various Dens of the Klan would interact with one another, carrying out acts of vengeance and violence in behalf of an earlier warning given to citizens within the boundaries of still another Klan Den.

In addition to the Klan's direct growth that particular year, a number of other similarly inclined secret white society groups began to appear in the Southern states. Among them was the White Camellia that was founded that same year in Franklin, Louisiana. Eventually the White Camellia established headquarters in New Orleans and extended membership to other Gulf States while the Klan extended its own membership further northward. Other groups that surfaced on occasion in latter 1860s were the White Brotherhood, the Pale Faces, and the Knights of the White Rose. While most of these organizations were never directly connected with the post Civil War Klu Klux Klan, many scholars later viewed them as well within the service of the Invisible Empire.

As the membership in the Klan and related organizations grew by the thousands in 1868 and early 1869 the acts of recorded violence unquestionably grew in seemingly exact accord with prospering of Dens. Certainly the criminal acts could have been committed at the time by still another group of masked terrorists, organized or otherwise, but the connection was hard to dismiss. An incident in 1868 Florida showed the Klan clearly at work. In May of that year Harrison Reed was elected governor amid bitter factional conflicts. Reed, formerly a newspaper publisher in Wisconsin, was clearly an advocate of sovereignty of the United States and a sworn enemy of the Klan. A few months after Reed took office the state legislature elected Adonijah S. Welsh to the United States Senate. Welsh, a Reed ally, had formerly lived in Michigan, and was then teaching black children in a Negro school in Florida. Welsh took office July of 1868 about the same time that Klan violence in that state grew more and more widespread. Rather than rely on Federal troops, which had been summoned to other southern states, Reed decided to form a new state militia to deal with the expanding Klan forces.

Part of Governor Reed's plan involved a shipment of two thousand rifles from the north to arm members of the Florida state militia. Apparently the Klan learned of the plan well in advance. On the night of November 6, 1868, as the train roared to Tallahassee somewhere between Lake City and Madison, the entire cargo of rifles were seized and tossed from the train. Reports immediately afterwards attributed the act to white "regulators".

Some years later United States Attorney General T.W. Gregory, in a speech before the Texas-Arkansas Bar Association, recalled the vivid details:

Robert M. Reed

"Every telegraph operator, brakeman, engineer and conductor on the road over which these arms entered the State was a Ku Klux; the shipment was watched at every point, and between Lake City and Madison the entire two carloads of guns were thrown from the moving train at night by a select band...who had quietly boarded the train at its last stop. The Ku Klux left the train at the next station and destroyed the shipment before it was missed, and this not withstanding the fact that two coaches filled with United States soldiers, sent to guard the arms, were attached to the same train."

While Grand Wizard Forrest insisted in a public speech the Klan was a "protective, political, military organization," newspaper accounts in prime Klan territories were telling a different story. Among the hundreds of news reports of lawless acts of violence at the time one stood out with particular chill and irony. The Chicago-Herald told of an incident in Savannah, Georgia:

"A mob lynched the wrong Negro at Eastman, it was learned last night. The victim was not Ed Clause, suspected of raping a schoolteacher, but a different young Negro. The real Clause was located near Darien yesterday.

"Before the lynching, the victim had protested that he was not Clause, had never met the school teacher and pleaded for time to prove his innocence.

"It is expected that the real Ed Clause will be lynched shortly."

Documentation by the Southern Poverty Law Center cites another example of many instances where local authorities, even when willing to stand-up to the Klan were not enough. In 1869 in Green County, Alabama prosecuting attorney Alexander Boyd declared his own war on the Klan terrorism. When three young black men were found dead in the countryside, the Klan was immediately suspected and Boyd declared that he knew the names of the guilty parties and further, would bring them to justice. On the following night, a band of more than 35 Klansmen rode into Eutaw to the inn when the prosecutor lived. They forced the night clerk to let them into Boyd's room, and then riddled his body with bullets, including two through the forehead. Then the Klansmen remounted their horses, circled the town square once for effect, and rode out of town. The epitaph on Boyd's tombstone could have applied to any number of people during those dark years. It read simply: "Murdered by the Ku Klux."

Situations like this, and involvement from the federal government caused Imperial Wizard Forrest to openly call for the disbandment of the Ku Klux Klan in 1869. Forrest also ordered all the Klan records to be destroyed, along with robes and other Klan memorabilia. Some historians suggest that Forrest gave the order simply to avoid further heat from federal authorities

Night of the Klan, A Reporter's Story

and dodge responsibility for an organization that was largely out of control. Whatever the Wizard's motives were, the Klan itself slowed somewhat in its activities as the year drew to a close.

"That the Invisible Empire had been dissolved by its Grand Wizard was not known publicly at the time, or indeed for long years afterward," noted Robert Henry in The Story of Reconstruction. "There were farewell parades of hooded riders and sheeted horses, as a gesture of defiance, but outside the ranks of the Klan itself no one knew that they were prelude to the destruction of regalia and records."

"To the outside world," Henry concluded, "activities of the sort ascribed to the Ku Klux continued, sporadically, while the very words and all that they conjured remained as part of the stock and trade of the Radical politician, in Congress and out."

Not everyone agreed with that assessment. And still others at the time argued that from that point only the more aggressive elements of the Klan were involved. On January 9, 1870 The New York World carried this account written by Miss Eliza Frances Andrews regarding the situation in Wilkes County, Georgia:

"When the Ku Klux Klan was first introduced into Georgia, it seemed more like a sort of organized practical joke upon the Negroes than any serious enterprise...But before long the low-downers took to Ku-Klucking as they call it, and then cruelties began to be practiced, and decent men withdrew from the organization altogether...Whenever a set of low, disorderly fellows feel inclined to commit a rascality, they put on masks and call themselves Ku Klux. A true statement of the case is not that the Ku Klux are an organized band of licensed criminals, but that men who commit crimes call themselves Ku Klux."

Congress took a darker view. They passed Force Acts in 1870 and 1871, plus the Ku Klux Klan Act of 1871 that authorized the president to use military force in necessary and declare martial law in areas where the orders were active. Early in 1872 a report of the Joint Select Committee of the House of Representatives declared the Klan remained "a fearful conspiracy against society...It has demoralized socially and held men silent by the terror of its acts and its powers for evil."

The report contained thousands of accounts of Klan inspired violence, destruction, and even murder. Whatever the nature of the Klan organizations, the aim of the most zealous was to prevent blacks from voting and if possible to prevent blacks from being educated in the South. Other groups such as the White League, Red Shirts, and similar groups acted similarly staging armed demonstrations in public and resorting to lawlessness in the dark of night. Teachers in particular remained targeted. Klan groups often appeared with armed force at those schools that dared to provide public education to black children. Accounts of teachers, both male and female, being threatened, assaulted or whipped in the 1870s were frequent. In many cases even the school houses were burned to the ground by Klan nightriders. Such acts of violence, even as the KKK was seemingly disbanded, were reported with frequency in Mississippi, Georgia and South Carolina.

With or without the Klan, whites of the Old South had generally returned to power by 1876, and once again controlled most the political operation within the original Confederate states. Early in 1877 President Rutherford Hayes used federal powers to entirely withdraw federal troops from the areas once threatened with dominance by the Ku Klux Klan. Despite outward appearances of being no longer a thriving organization, the Klan had left a lasting impression on the decade of the 1870s. Future attorney general Gregory described the Klan at the time as "the most thoroughly organized, extensive and effective vigilance committee the world has ever seen, or it's likely to see." Had Gregory been able to foresee the 20th century and newer versions of the Klu Klux Klan he would have not make the dramatic statement.

Generally speaking the direct activities of the Klan subsided during the 1880s. Perhaps as Klan Report of The Southern Poverty Law Center summarized the end of the 19th century, "the Klu Klux Klan's brief grip on the South (had) faded, and its bloody deeds were forgotten by many whites who were once in sympathy with its cause." Perhaps Klan members and Klan supports no longer felt the threat of federal forces or for the time being did not feel the threat of any accession to power by black citizens.

Still there was the formation of various 'white power' groups including the formation of the American Protective Association in 1887, and the Whitecaps the following year. While these groups also avowed racism and were bound by secret oaths they differed only slightly from the 'old' Klan in that their hostility was directed at immigrants as well as blacks. And their geographical region was more Midwestern and reached even into parts of the Northwest.

The New Century

Some would credit the media for putting the flame to the fiery cross of the Ku Klux Klan in the early dawn of the 20th century. It began with a book.

Thomas Dixon was a southern-based minister and strong advocate of Christian white supremacy who felt the written word added to the impact of his personal preaching. Dixon wrote several papers advocating his views

Night of the Klan, A Reporter's Story

and eventually turned to moralistic novels. His second novel, The Clansman, written in 1905 became a best seller.

Basically the book presented the Klan of the 19th century as a kindly brotherhood of peacemakers who rescued the Old South from ignorant blacks and arrogant Federal authorities. In that time and climate the public in general enjoyed the simplistic story of The Clansman. Wyn Craig, author of the distinguished book The Fiery Cross, noted in his study of Dixon that the minister who eventually migrated to the North with his teachings found willing followers:

"His race baiting was not unusual in the turn of the century (1900s) America. Pseudoscientific works on the inferiority of blacks had already found wide audiences. But Dixon was unique. The degree to which he saw the difference between good and evil determined entirely by race was unrivaled until Mein Kampf; and his delusions and fears would have fit comfortably among the case studies in Psychopatia Sexualis."

Interestingly as popular as the book was at the time, efforts to convert The Clansman into a successful stage play failed and the concept no doubt would have fallen into obscurity had it not been for a rising young star in a place called Hollywood.

For whatever reasons motion picture director D.W. Griffith liked the book and was convinced it would make a thrilling movie. One particular appealing aspect for moviemaker Griffith was the book's overview of the South being saved from barbarism by the Knights of the Klu Klux Klan. As the novel observed they were the likes "the world had not seen since the Knights of the Middle Ages rode on their Holy Crusades." That image would translate into an immortal movie in Griffith's mind. It that sense Griffith was right. In fact nearly a century later movie critics and historians generally agree that the Griffith movie was—from a production standpoint—excellent. The movie premiered before a packed house in Los Angeles on January 8, 1915. Immediately after the premiere the movie was rewarded with a more sweeping title, The Birth of A Nation. While the movie was generally well received, the newly formed National Association for the Advancement of Colored People protested it declaring the film depicted "Negroes in the worst possible light." Of course it did, but nobody beyond the NAACP seemed offended by the glaring racial stereotyping and glorification of the Ku Klux Klan.

The book's author Thomas Dixon reappeared on the national scene in February of that year by appealing directly to President Woodrow Wilson to say something nice about the film. Wilson of course had never seen the movie nor had he read much about it. Reviews had been mostly good, including one New York newspaper, which proclaimed, "If there is a greater picture than Birth of a Nation, may we live to see it." What won over

Wilson however was not the reviews but his kinship to Dixon who had been a friend back in his college days at John Hopkins University. Wilson refused to go out to a public theatre because he was still in mourning for his late wife. However he agreed to a private showing of the film in the White House. The private showing on February 18, 1915 must have been quite a sight. There with President Wilson were author Dixon, movie director Griffith and a host of Washington powers including the Chief Justice of the Supreme Court. Watching white Klansmen do battle with the evil black militia in the streets of the Old South was inspiring to the Washington crowd. The Klan's "parade of liberators" made a very dramatic ending for the eager viewers. Dixon said the presentation was designed "to revolutionize northern sentiment by presentation of history that would transform every man in my audience...And make no mistake about it—we are doing just that." President Wilson seemed to agree.

"It is like writing history with lighting, and my only regret is that it is all so true," said the President after the viewing.

Most other members of the elite audience were also pleased, as was the National Board of Censorship, which approved the film by a vote of 15 to eight a few days later in New York City. Looking back historian James Loewen observed that Birth of a Nation "was a landmark of American cinema, not only was it the best technical production of this time but also probably the most racist major movie of all time."

Quite apart from the silver screen that year was a third player named William Joseph Simmons. Rather than a media background, Simmons had a military background being a veteran of the Spanish-American War. In the late fall of the same year as the premiere of The Birth of the Nation, Simmons took charge over an actual re-birth of the Ku Klux Klan. Simmons gathered a group of about 30 or 40 white males at a Georgia location on Stone Mountain, not too distant from Atlanta. The 'new' century Klan was based to a large extent on the 19th century Klan groups but the targets of their hatred had been updated to include not only blacks but also Catholics and Jews, plus most any foreign-born citizens. Besides taking the title of Imperial Wizard, Simmons also decided to take the title of Colonel not because he had ever held that military rank but because, as he later recalled, it was a term used at the time for lawyers in Georgia and he felt it would give him greater status. Accounts say Imperial Wizard Simmons closed the first Klan meeting of the new century by burning a giant cross of pinecones. A short time later on December 4, 1915, the state of Georgia granted a charter to the newly formed Knights of the Ku Klux Klan.

Even with the popularity of The Birth of A Nation movie, which played in movie houses across America, early growth was slow for the new Klan. For one thing, there were other so-called benevolent organizations already appealing to white males for membership. And for another, the Klan group lacked both promotional skills and the ability to protect its own finances.

"For three years the work was a tremendous struggle," Simmons later testified under oath, "made more arduous by a traitor in the ranks who embezzled all of our accumulate funds in the summer of 1916 and went off and attempted to organize a counterfeit order. The treasonous conduct of the man left me penniless, with large accumulated debts against the order... I was forced to mortgage my home to get money with which to carry on the fight against this traitor's counterfeit order and to assist in the work we had to do."

At one point Klan insider J.B. Frost suggested a plan to Imperial Wizard Simmons to help the group's financial difficulties and to more or less 'share' leadership of the organization. Frost's plan to Simmons called for Frost to appoint an imperial staff of six officers, which would attend to the details of the Klan. In return Simmons would be given $30,000 in cash and would retain the title of Imperial Wizard. Simmons declined the offer and Klan membership languished. Indeed the 'new' Klan may well have disappeared much quicker than the old Klan had it not been for the intervention of a pair of public relation wheel-dealers from Atlanta. Edward Young and Elizabeth Tyler had enjoyed some moderate success through conducting fund-raising drives for various organizations as the South Publicity Association. Young was said to have a hand in conducting campaigns for such unlikely causes as the Roosevelt Memorial Association and the Near East Relief. Some said that Young and Tyler simply applied the earlier techniques used in successful World War I drives from Liberty Loan to food conservation to sell the Klan to the American public. At any rate the duo and Imperial Wizard Simmons were finally on the same page.

As they saw it there was money to be made in future Klan membership drives if only the group would stress more "fellowship" and "fraternal" rather than their very overt appeals to racism. They suggested also that the Klan play-down anti-Catholic and anti-Jewish references at least as far as membership drives were concerned. On the other hand the 'old' Klan usage of secret ceremonies, cross burnings, and wearing of hoods and robes could be good for business. Young and Tyler considered them to be very sellable items. They predicted a "wonderful revival" of the Klan and they proved to be right. Reportedly Imperial Wizard immediately set about refining and defining the 'new' Klan in a more positive light. Selected targets of the Klan were expanded to include Asians, with continued emphasis of the threat on any 'foreign-born' immigrants. For good measure the Klan also pledged itself to be equally at war with roadhouses, illegal drugs, and immoral behavior in general. The newly refurbished Ku Klux Klan promised a sort of social vigilance up front, but yet strongly hinted some kind of secret vengeance beneath costumed hoods and robes.

Some accounts said the team of Young and Tyler got a shocking eighty percent of all membership fees for their assistance and direction. Other accounts suggest the agreement was perhaps more complicated and further involved a share of an additional initiation fee, plus a part of any robe sales. Whatever share eventually went to the Southern Publicity Association, no doubt Imperial Wizard Simmons thought it was a very good deal. From that point on until the end of September in the following year the Klan raised more than $860,000. Since the Klan was pitching itself as a benevolent society that revenue and the vast amounts that followed were considered to be tax free. This 'tax free' status of exploding amounts of money eventually prompted a federal investigation of their mail solicitations but at the time it certainly did not discourage those within the Klan organization.

During that dramatic growth period the Simmons' Klan expanded from bases in Alabama, Louisiana, South Carolina, Mississippi, and Florida to having Klaverns in at least 45 states including much of the Midwest. In the overview of the Klan commercial operation the nation was divided into Domains, which were then subdivided into Realms. Simmons maintained the title of Imperial Wizard. Business consultant Young became the Imperial Kleagle, while co-consultant Tyler being the lone female was given no title at all. Meanwhile in near corporate fashion the Domains were directed by Grand Goblins and the Realms were placed under the supervision of King Kleagles. On down the line were assorted Genii, Grand Titans, Furies, Exalted Cyclops, and so forth. Not only did the titles add to the glitz and glamour of the organization, they further served to collect and distribute what became a remarkable amount of money.

Simply put the Klan of the 1920s had something earlier Klan organizations had decidedly lacked before—a profit motive. Membership to those willing to take the oath was $10. Of that significant fee for the times, four dollars when into the pocket of the local Kleagle and another one dollar went to the King Kleagel. Meanwhile the Grand Goblin took fifty cents of the initial fee while others sometimes allotted smaller amounts. Ultimately four dollars arrived at Klan headquarters in Atlanta where Imperial Kleagle Young and Tyler cut themselves a share of $2.50 for each membership. Thousands of members were signed up into membership and tens of thousands of dollars rolled into the upraised palms of the Klan hierarchy. At one point early in Roaring Twenties decade federal postal authorities determined that the Ku Klux Klan, once struggling for membership, now had paid King Kleagles in more than 40 states, plus at least nine Grand Goblins, all working fulltime for the cause (and the profits) of the Invisible Empire.

Night of the Klan, A Reporter's Story

(And the distribution of membership fees did not begin to include another hefty $6.50 local Klans charged for traditional uniform robes. The robe business itself became so profitable that the KKK not content with a part of the profits, they eventually acquired the entire robe manufacturing operations themselves.).

As the Klan grew their appeal became somewhat regionalized. Literature distributed in the South hinted at a widespread "Negro uprising", but in other parts of country the group stressed a "planned take-over" of the country by Catholics and Jews. Not surprisingly incidents of violence grew as Klan membership grew. The number of floggings, whippings, and the lynching continued to be reported in greater numbers by newspapers in the South and to an extent in the Midwest. Of course it was likely that many, if not most, of the freely performed acts of violence were never reported by a any newspaper much less by an law enforcement agency. By and large newspapers ignored directly linking the Ku Klux Klan of the early 1920s with the violence, which became more and more common throughout the countryside. Some newspapers feared the Klan, and some newspapers supported the Klan. A very few newspapers were willing to fully take on the Klan, among them were the Memphis Commercial appeal in Memphis, Tennessee, and Montgomery Advertiser in Montgomery, Alabama and the New York World in New York City.

As early as October of 1920 the New York daily was drawing attention to the growing membership of the Klan. On October 10, 1920 a World story datelined from Atlanta, Georgia began as follows:

"The old Ku Klux Klan of Reconstruction days has been revived. Hooded night-riders in long, flowing white gowns parade the thoroughfares and bypaths of the South in the dark hours when innocent people are abed."

To be sure it was not only the "bypaths of the South" when the Klan was rising to power. It became ever powerful in the bypaths of much of the rest of the United States. Even conservative estimates put membership in the millions during the decade of the 1920s as the hatred marketed with memberships varied somewhat with the region of the country. The California Klan of the 1920s was largely anti-Japanese and anti-Chinese, the Oregon Klan was mainly anti-Catholic, the Klan of the Midwest was mainly anti-black and anti-Catholic, and some of the Klans in eastern states centered their hatred against Jews and political liberals. As one journalist observed at the time, the Klan "suited its hates to the local market." The local market extended to significant political control of states like Oregon, Oklahoma, Texas, Arkansas, Alabama, Indiana, Ohio and even much of California. Moreover the Klan benefited from its own secrecy violence. Wherever an act of midnight terrorism was carried out on some defenseless victim the KKK was credited and such tales in turn added to the mysticism.

Violence begot violence and often the Klan was given unwarranted credit for isolated terrorism in a community what would have been unlikely to blame anyone else. Klan or not it was an easy way to pass off the blame and thus protect otherwise good-standing citizens. Ironically the KKK itself was in some communities the strongest force known and easily thwarted or simply intimidated local law enforcement. There were hundreds of cases where seemingly otherwise good people would turn to town Klan leadership to punish—rightfully or not—neighbors or even passing strangers.

In September 1921 the New York World began an elaborate series of articles designed to expose the ever- powerful Ku Klux Klan. To give the series further impact it was syndicated to 18 other daily newspapers around the United States including the St. Louis Post-Dispatch, the Boston Globe, the Pittsburgh Sun, and the Cleveland Plain-Dealer. Among other things the articles documented that the Klan had more than 200 active recruiting offices stretching from Atlanta to Los Angeles. The World also pointed out that both Tyler and Young of the Southern Publicity Association had been arrested during a raid on a house of prostitution some years earlier. Both were found guilty of disorderly conduct. Decades later the Special Klan Report of the Southern Poverty Law Center would say that the World accounts "badly tarnished the Klan's moralistic image and began a serious rift within the ranks." Moreover it caused Congress to launch a Washington-based investigation of the Klan. The Imperial Wizard Simmons himself was called before the Committee on Rules of the House of Representatives. In elaborate remarks Simmons denied any Klan involvement in violent acts attributed them in various parts of the United States. Further, the Imperial Wizard said the "attacks against the Klan were originated and started by the New York World, which is owned and controlled by a Jew, Mr. Pulitzer, whose main purpose is circulation and revenue."

Yet despite any 'rifts' and despite the Congressional hearings, not only was the Klan movement not immediately harmed, but it likely caused it to grow stronger. One skeptic historian even noted that if the newspaper series added to the World's circulation by 100,000 it may have also increased the direct Klan membership by many thousand. Of course the House Committee took no action against the Klan leadership either. The Klan continued on the march and Imperial Wizard Simmons seemed well pleased with the direction it was heading. The newspaper series and the Congressional hearings apparently did little to hold black the flood of membership. Early in 1922 Simmons told The New York Times that the organization was now accepting new members at the rate of 3,500 per day and further that it had taken in more than 16 million dollars annually in initiation fees and sale of robes and hoods. At that point, according to the Klan chieftain, the group had membership in all 48 states, plus the Territory of Alaska and the Panama Canal Zone.

Simmons boasted the KKK had a membership of five million members in 1922. Of course the figure could have been somewhat of an exaggeration, but it is not likely. Some remarkable research by Paul Gillette and Eugene Tillinger for the book Inside The Ku Klux Klan established Klan membership in the middle 1920s at somewhere near the nine million mark. They suggest as many as one of eight American males between the ages of 21 and 65 was enrolled.

These are astonishing figures in light of the fact that many American males in this age at the time were actually "ineligible to join because they were Jewish, Negro, Catholic, or foreign-born."

To perhaps visualize the full effect of the organization's membership, one newspaper account at the time might be helpful. In May of 1923 the New York World again drew attention to the Ku Klux Klan. Here is the account of a Klan rally not in a southern state or even a border state, but at a location near New Brunswick, New Jersey. The account spoke of the departure:

"Then a dark column of men poured through a gap in the line. From a distance of three hundred feet they looked like a huddled flock of frightened herded prisoners. The committeeman told us there were two thousand of them."

After the Klan rally cars left the dark night in all directions.

"At half-pass three o'clock this morning automobiles were still going through New Brunswick like traffic at Forty Second Street and Broadway at three o'clock in the afternoon."

During the previous November the figurative leadership torch of the Klan had been taken rather dramatically by Texas dentist Hiram Wesley Evans. To be exact Evans was originally from Alabama but moved to Texas to establish a dental practice at the end of World War I. Evans rose from the position of Exalted Cyclops of Dallas to become Great Titan of the Realm of Texas early in 1922. In the months that followed Evans managed to get himself appointed to the rank if Imperial Kligrapp or national secretary by Imperial Wizard Simmons. It proved to be a good career move for Evans and a rather poor one for Simmons.

As the national secretary of the organization Evans was more or less free to travel various states and built his own personal base within the overall Klan. His strongest 'traveling' ally soon became Midwestern Klan official David Curtis Stephenson. Stephenson was based in Indiana but had substantial contacts and influence in Michigan, Ohio, Illinois and other surrounding states. Other members of the insurgent Klan group included Brown Harwood of Texas, James Comer of Arkansas, and Nathan Bedford

Forrest, Jr. of Georgia the son of the noted Confederate officer who was credited with being the original leader of the 1860s Ku Klux Klan.

By November of that year Doc Evans and sidekick Stephenson had rounded-up enough support to totally control the Klan national convention in Atlanta. Just to be sure Stephenson and New York Klan leader Fred Savage made a pre-dawn visit to Imperial Wizard Simmons. Stephenson and Savage, who now held the rank of chief of the Klan's Department of Investigation, grimly told the wizard there might be enough armed guards to protect him as the convention took place, but the situation looked risky at best. An option, they told a worried Simmons, would be to make a deal and give his full support to Doc Evans as the new Imperial Wizard. In turn Simmons would avoid possibly being shot by disgruntled Klansmen, and he would be given the new title of Klan Emperor. Simmons immediately took the deal.

"Well," Simmons later confided to others about the 4 a.m. meeting with Stephenson and Savage, "I didn't sleep any more than night."

Regardless of any structural changes the lawlessness and violence of the Klan continued unabated throughout the 1920s much of the United States. It was summed up in part by an editorial that ran in the New York Herald Tribune during the height of the Klan terrorism:

"When a mob of masked men invades a citizen's home at night, renders him helpless and then takes his wife out of bet, ties her to a barrel in the front yard and flogs her, is there any punishment within the law too drastic for the crime? We doubt it."

And to those who read and surmised such acts would take place only in the backwater towns of the Old South, there was this comment before a Congressional committee by C. Anderson Wright the King Kleagle of the New York Klan. In his sworn testimony Kleagle Wright recalled that Imperial Wizard Simmons promised the Klan would have 10,000 members in New York City alone, "and if we do not want a man to do a certain thing, he is not very apt to do it."

The Middle Years

William Joseph Simmons, once fondly known as the Colonel among his Klan comrades, never made it to the lofty rank of Klan Emperor. Dealing with the likes of Doc Evans and D.C. Stephenson he was lucky to make any kind of deal at all. Early in 1924 Colonel Simmons was able to make a financial settlement with Doc Evans and the new order Klan. As part of the deal Simmons relinquished all titles, copyrights, and even the charter of the ts of the Ku Klux Klan, Inc. One of the first official acts of Doc Evans

Night of the Klan, A Reporter's Story

and the 'new' Klan was to shift the headquarters of the Invisible Empire from Atlanta to Washington D.C. Among other things Evans sought to make the Invisible Empire more visible and more political as well. He and Stephenson reasoned that their vast membership could indeed influence the outcome of certain elections given the proper motivation and organization. They immediately set out to build such political influence in statewide races in Alabama, Georgia, California, Colorado, Indiana, Oklahoma, Ohio, and other states. As a rule the Klan members of the Old South tended to support Democrats while the Klan members in the northern and western states tended to support Republicans. Party did not matter to the new Klan nearly as much as getting involved in the political process of it all.

The farming community was a major membership target for 1920s Klan leaders of operating in the Middle West and other semi rural regions. Writing later in The Great Depression author Robert Goldston observed:

"In their frustration and growing anger, many farmers turned to older, more primitive views of the world. Thus, during the 1920s, the Ku Klux Klan, little more than a memory in the South, saw a rebirth in the Midwest. Klan ritual and Klan hatred of foreigners and minorities found a disturbingly wide response among farmers, who vaguely felt that the rest of the country was conspiring to keep them poor."

Meanwhile, Stephenson sat his own masterful example of political power with the 1924 governor's race in his home state of Indiana. When Stephenson and his fellow Klansmen backed Ed Jackson for governor the candidate swept to victory carrying 90 of Indiana's 92 counties.

Ironically the election victory was beginning of the end for Stephenson who often bragged, "I am the law in Indiana." During the governor's inaugural ball in January of 1925 the Klan leader became enchanted with a 28-year-old single statehouse office worker. When his telephone calls to the young lady were unsuccessful in the weeks that followed, Stephenson dispatched some of his Klan guards to bring the women to him. Forced aboard a northbound train from Indianapolis to northern Indiana, the woman was sexually assaulted and mutilated. Briefly freed, she used the money Stephenson had given her for a new hat to buy herself poison. Two days later the victim of Stephen's brutal assault died. Eventually the Indiana Grand Dragon and one of the Imperial Wizard's number one lieutenant was arrested and, after a much-publicized trail, was given a lengthy prison term. His handpicked governor made no effort to intercede.

Meanwhile the Klan violence continued unabated. Lynching, shootings and whippings were commonplace in communities throughout the country. Typically the lawless acts occurred when the Klan existed in substantial numbers and held enough political influence to assure little or no interference from law enforcement officers,

Of this period in American history the Special Report of the Ku Klux Klan, The Southern Poverty Law Center carefully noted:

"Such instances were not confined to the South—in Oklahoma Klansmen applied the lash to girls caught riding in automobiles with young men, and very early in the Klan revival women were flogged and even tortured in the San Joaquin Valley in California."

On a hot August day in 1925 Doc Evans may have reached the zenith of his reign. After months of planning the Ku Klux Klan marched 40,000 strong down Pennsylvania Avenue in Washington D.C. In lines nearly as far as the eye could see they streamed white-robed all the way to the George Washington Monument. Yet for all of this grandeur the great Washington parade may in reality have marked the passing of one of major Klan eras. By the following year Doc Evans could command only half the number of Klansman to enact a similar parade. In 1927 a group of renegade Klan members in Pennsylvania renounced the Evans' brand of Invisible Empire to form their own group. The Imperial Wizard filed a major lawsuit against them and bitter court battle ensued. Both sides, to pardon a phrase, were tarred by one another. Eventually, after a great deal of embarrassing publicity, the case brought by Doc Evans was dismissed.

Beyond the Doc Evans blunderings, times were simply changing.

In the immortal book Only Yesterday by Frederick Lewis Allen this remarkable period of transition was briefly described:

"Slowly, as the years passed and the war-time (World War I) emotions ebbed, the power of the Klan waned, until in many districts it was dead and in others it had become merely a political faction dominated by spoils men: but not until it had become a thing of terror to millions of men and women."

If the Klan had almost disappeared by the end of the 1920s, it was probably for a number of reasons. Allen offered a number including the waning of post World War I angers, and the second thoughts of some "who had joined the Klan from unselfish if ignorant motives and were dismayed to find it coming under the grip of local thugs and swindlers." Moreover the constant drumbeat of violence attributed to Klan nightriders was beginning to take its toll with the general public, encouragingly a great many people no longer had the stomach for such lawless behavior disguised beneath the bed sheets of the Invisible Empire. A drastically declining economy helped in its awful way as well, otherwise willing Klans members were no longer able to meet the regular cost of membership dues. Concludes Allen, "when the depression came along, the dues-paying membership shrank to almost nothing."

Early in the 1930s Klan leaders vainly attempted to redirect their organized hatred to also include the administration of President Franklin Roosevelt. The Klan openly complained about too many Catholics and Jews

Night of the Klan, A Reporter's Story

being involved in the federal government. Klan Imperial Wizard Evans also began making public comments about the threat of unions and communists. In general Klan membership appeared to decline nationally. Not only was there a social change about the country, but an economic one as well. The impact of the Great Depression forced great numbers of laboring men to ultimately focus on the survival of finding work rather than finding 'offenders' to punish.

All this is not to say Klan violence did not take place. It clearly did. In October of 1933 the New York Times reported this horrifying event in a place called Princess Anne, Maryland. It seemed a Klan-inspired lynch mob drug a black prisoner from a jail cell and lynched the poor man in front of the home of a judge who had earlier tired to calm the mob.

"The mob cut down the body, dragged it through the main thoroughfare for more than half a mile, and tossed it onto a burning pyre. Fifty state policemen and deputies battled vainly with the crowd, tossing tear-gas bombs in an effort to disperse it. Five policemen were beaten to the ground and the others were swept aside by the fury of townsmen and farmers, who had used a heavy wooden battering ram to smash three doors and reach the cell of the terrified prisoner, George Armwood, 24 years old."

The newspaper account continued:

"Despite the presence of women and children, his clothes were torn form his body and he was hanged nude. One boy, about 18 years old, slashed off the Negro's ear with a knife."

For some reason Florida in the 1930s was one of the few states where the Klan retained much of the power and structure that it had maintained in the 1920s. Reports regarding Klan membership in the Sunshine state put the figure at well over 30,000 early in the decade of the 1930s. Very active klaverns were being noted in the so-called citrus belt from Orlando to Tampa. There was similar Klan activity in Miami, Jacksonville, and in select parts of isolated northwestern Florida. Scarcely a week after the lynching incident in Maryland was reported, another newspaper account grimly documented a similar act of violence in Marianna, Florida. According to the Birmingham Post a black man, 23, was suspected of attacking a white girl. After being strung up to a tree limb his body was then lowered for the mob to take further vengeance.

"A woman related to the murdered girl drove a butcher knife into his heart. Then the crowd came by and some kicked him and some drove their cars over him.

"What remained of the body was brought by the mob to Marianna where it now hangs from a tree on the northeast corner of the courthouse square."

While these violent acts continued into the middle and latter 1930s the overall membership and consequently the political strength of the Klan continued to dwindle. Besides all the reasons mentioned previously, there was also a matter of the emergence of other right-wing fringe groups. Active groups now included the Knights of the White Camellia organized by George Deatherage, the German-American Bund led by Fritz Kuhn, and The Silver Shirts under the leadership of William Dudley Pelly. Based in North Carolina, the very Klan-like white-supremacy Silver Shirts eventually grew in numbers to about 15,000. At the time one printed commentary suggested the Silver Shirt were simply a "great shift form sheets to shirts." While the Silver Shirts eventually made some inroads with their anti-Jewish tracts, the group never reached the heights of the prior Ku Klux Klan groups.

During 1934 and 1935 there were reports from Georgia that Doc Evans was again trying to put life back into the crumbling Klan. Besides the usual racial and religious hate there was spoken sympathies with political movements in Germany and the offer to fight communism. Overall the so-called revival was a feeble one. News accounts regularly noted the flight of middle-class white males to groups like the Silver Shirts and a host of other seemingly more appealing extremist groups including the Black Legion that was based in Michigan.

In 1937 when it was disclosed that newly appointed United States Supreme Court justice Hugo Black had joined the Ku Klux Klan back in 1926, there was public concern that the 'old Klan' might rise again. It had, by most accounts, after all helped Black win earlier election to the United States Senate. Did the Klan now own a Supreme Court justice, and was a new reign of terror about to begin? In the fall of that year the powerful Literary Digest seem to take that question head-on in a major article on the Klan. It was again just possible "some other Klan" would sweep the country into a new form of fascism concluded the magazine, "for we are a lawless and impatient people, tolerance comes hard to many of us."

The Literary Digest of October 9, 1937 continued, "we have millions of people living in dire want, and our economic problems are of such immense size and complexity that the spellbinder who can provide a scapegoat to be punished, or a flag-draped panacea to be adopted, can collect hundreds of thousands of witless followers." But the magazine suggested the best protection for the country could be a sense of humor.

"Kleagles and Grand Goblins may make terrifying headway among us for a time—but in due course that laughter which is the beginning of wisdom in likely to begin."

With all due respect to the once highly noted magazine it was doubtful that many Americans were about to enter the next decade laughing. There was little humor in the overall Great Depression of the 1930s, much less in the hate-filled doctrine of the Klan and similar groups. Like it or not sill "another" Klan was about to be unleashed and humor would be in very short supply. This time yet another 'new' Klan would involve itself with the changing times and turmoil Europe. Mounting divisions in America would open fertile fields for a slightly altered brand of klanism. Some of the anti-Catholic fervor of the past, for one thing, was toned down. The biggest change however was the Klan flirtation was Nazi Germany. The relationship would fully blossom in the 1940s.

At still another special Klan klanvocation in the city of Atlanta Imperial Wizard Doc Evans finally surrendered the KKK reigns to an assistant who had served with him during the previous two years. The Klan's new Imperial Wizard for the 1940s was James Arnold Colescott, a veterinarian from Terre Haute, Indiana.

The War Years 1940s

At some point just before Doc Evans had relinquished control of the Klan organization he was made a serious financial offer by leaders in the National Workers League, a growing pro-Nazi labor organization. The Klan and the NWL had a growing mutual relationship as early as the late 1930s. Moreover the foreign powers that controlled the NWL foresaw an even greater role for the rank and file of America's remaining Invisible Empire.

During a secret meeting in 1939 the Nazi-controlled American Phalanx organization decreed a new relationship with the Ku Klux Klan. American Phalanx, previously identified as the political Christian Front, disclosed the revised policy before members who met in the cellar of a tavern near 125th Street and Eighth Avenue in New York City. In the book Under Cover, My Four Years in the Nazi Underworld of America, John Ray Carlson explained that the announced Phalanx directive was based on "orders from General Headquarters to expand and consolidate with every nationalist group in town."

At the meeting a Phalanx leader explained the Klan connection, in part, this way:

"In the South the Klan is anti-Catholic, but in the North it's only anti-Jewish. We will ride in blood, spreading confusion and terror in the Jew. Not little Ikey Moscowitz who keeps a stationery store, but the big Jews. You don't have to think how it will be done. We don't want you to think. We'll do you thinking for you."

Not surprisingly Imperial Wizard Evans was soon after offered $75,000 from a collective of Nazi-collected groups in return for controlling interest in the Klan organization. Evans passed on the offer but the new Imperial Wizard James Arnold Colescott saw things quite differently when he took charge of the Klan a short time later. Colescott immediately reversed Klan tradition to warm to the American labor movement. Before the Klan had generally denounced organized labor but in the dawn of the 1940s decade—like Nazi influences in America—leaders such as Colescott began to see the potential of dividing if not directly attracting union members.

At one point Imperial Wizard Colescott told his followers:

"Get into every (union) local, every department, division and plant...The UAW (United Auto Workers) and CIO leaders are all Reds. We must Americanize them though Kluxing every white, Protestant, Gentile American."

In Detroit, Michigan the Klan worked hand-in-hand with the Nazi party to secure leadership positions in key labor unions. Wherever possible the Klan advocated disruptions in production, wildcat strikes, and other actions to directly hinder the war effort. The Klan openly campaigned against the union's Victory Program and attempted to halt union participation in the sale of U.S. Defense Bonds.

Klan penetration took on serious proportions early in the 1940s at Detroit's Packard automotive plant where marine and aircraft motors were being manufactured both for American and British armed forces. The Klan exerted every effort at that time to infiltrate the union there by actively recruiting the work force. On August 18, 1940 the Ku Klux Klan staged what one report called a "monster anti-war, pro-American mass meeting" near Andover, New Jersey. In case anyone had not noticed the fact before, the site was carefully selected to mark the obvious connection with the Klan and the Nazi Party. The location was the Nazi Camp Nordland where a 40-foot wooden cross would be burned late than evening.

More than 3,500 Klansmen and German American Bundists were assembled that hot summer afternoon, the Klan in their traditional white robes and the Bundists in their military-like gray uniforms. The anti-Catholic line, implied and just about promised by the Phalanx organization earlier, was clear at the rally. Declared one Klan speaker:

"Whatever power or money the Jews had, has been confiscated. But a world-wide militant Catholic organization directed from Rome remains a sinister threat to our Americanism."

A speaker representative of the German-American Bund addressed the crowd assuring, "the principals of the Bund and the principals of the Klan are the same."

Later that year another major Klan rally was conducted in Rockford, Illinois. This time the Klan joined forces with the American First Committee in an effort to raise funds and recruit membership. Thousands of Klansmen appeared at the rally, which launched a familiar sounding "Americanization program" which was designed to raise one million dollars. A featured speaker at the Klan rally was Senator C. Wayland Brooks. Further to the

Night of the Klan, A Reporter's Story

north in Detroit, Klan efforts to increase membership in the ranks of union members began to show some signs of success. At least the National Workers League remained convinced of their relative strength.

In 1941 pro-Nazi Parker Sage, a leader of the National Workers League, contacted undercover agent Carlson in an attempt to lure him into the Detroit effort. Sage told Carlson the Klan there "was decidedly a strong factor here...and has, as far as we can learn, confined themselves to the Racial Problem-Jew and Negro." The NWL regularly reprinted and distributed Klan literature at that time in Detroit. Before joining the NWL organization in Detroit, Carlson made visits to Court Asher the publisher of the subversive X Ray published in Muncie, Indiana and to Illinois Klan leader Gale S. Carter who shared offices in Rockford, Illinois with the NWL and other groups. In Muncie, Asher confided to Carlson he used to be a Klan member, "but I gave that up."

Once in Detroit agent Carlson reported contact with a Michigan autoworker and many others who were members of both the NWL and the Ku Klu Klan. He distributed literature for both groups among the workers of the Ford plant in the Motor City. The worker explained to Carlson, "I have an audience every lunch hour." Elsewhere in Detroit the Klan and the NWL managed to incite full-scale rioting in places like the Sojourner Truth Settlement. At the Settlement, a defense housing project was designated by the United States Housing Authority "for occupancy by Negro defense workers and their families," Klan militants set up blockades to stop blacks from entering the project. Dozens of people were injured in the ensuing fighting.

A chilling effect on Klan activities nationwide took place in July of 1942 when the United States Department of Justice indicted 28 individuals, 30 publications and a number of national organizations including the Silver Shirts, German American Bund, National Workers League, and the Ku Klux Klan. The Grand Jury, meeting in Washington, D.C., charged the Klan with specific attempts to sabotage American morale. Just a few months earlier the Trial Board of the United Auto Workers attracted national attention when it moved to expel Klansman Frank Buehrle from the union. The board ruled Buehrle was guilty of "actively building the Ku Klux Klan" in the Packard automotive plant, and of attempting to sabotage the morale of Packard workers.

With World War II fully raging, and federal charges pending, the 1940s scope of the Ku Klux Klan was considerably blunted. Major rallies and fund-raising efforts all but disappeared. In January of 1943 a small advertisement appeared in the Enterprise newspaper of Maryville, Tennessee. In an effort to rekindle the fires of previous years it read:

"Wanted: 5,000 or more of the 10,000 Klansmen in the following counties answers this ad: Knox, Blount, Monroe, and Loudon—there is work to do. Write Klansman, Box No. 30."

It is doubtful that the response was all that great. By the following year the Internal Revenue Service had built up enough evidence against the national Ku Klux Klan organization to file a lien in federal court against the Invisible Empire for $685,000 in back taxes. Imperial Wizard Colescott was outwardly devastated by the news. Shortly after the IRS suit's full impact in 1944, leader Colescott lamented openly, "we (the Klan) had to sell our assets and hand over the proceeds to the government and go out of business. Maybe the government can make something out of the Klan—-I never could."

The end of World War II in the middle of 1945 was probably good news for every citizen and organization in America except for the Ku Klux Klan and a few others. World war and world peace had brought significant social and political change in the United States. The country welcomed a wave of new immigrants, Jewish refugees arrived daily, soldiers who had served on distant shores now regularly returned home with foreign-born "war brides". Black soldiers meanwhile, nearly a million of them, who had seen life in the military and in the strife of war often returned with a much different view of the world and the United States.

In December of 1946 President Harry Truman appointed a committee to investigate and report on the status of civil rights in American. Truman clearly hoped to prevent a revival of the Klan that had occurred shortly after the end of World War I and lasted for a decade. The steadfast committee recommended sweeping changes including an anti-lynching law; abolition of the poll tax; laws ending discrimination in voter registration; and an end to segregation in the armed forces. The Truman administration also established a Fair Employment Practices Commission, created a permanent Commission on Civil Rights, and mandated a Civil Rights Division in the Justice Department.

For all of these reasons, and more, the Klan continued to rapidly decline in as a force in the dwindling years of the 1940s decade. For a time there were stirrings from within the Klan. In Atlanta, Georgia physician Samuel Green renewed recruiting efforts and managed to temporarily revise interest in places like Kentucky, New York, New Jersey, and Pennsylvania as well as in southern states like Tennessee, South Carolina, Alabama and Florida. However despite Dr. Green's efforts and finances widespread interest never materialized. When the doctor died in 1949 the old Klan was in decided ill health as well,

By 1950 most accounts put the membership of the Ku Klux Klan at perhaps its lowest ebb since it beginning of the 20th Century back on Stone

Mountain. In 1953 an automotive worker in Atlanta, Georgia once again attempted to revise the Klan organization. The efforts of Eldon Edwards were identified as the U.S. Klans of the Knights of the Ku Klux Klan.

The meager effort would have likely remained obscure has it not been for a United States Supreme Court ruling less than 12 months later. In dramatic action the Supreme Court ruled in 1954 that "separate but equal" was not an acceptable status in the country's public schools. Instead full integration of black and white school children was necessary. Such a ruling immediately served to inflame hard-core segregationists including former Klansmen and potential new members of the Invisible Empire. By 1956 the Edwards led group had grown strong enough to hold a major rally at the historically familiar Stone Mountain in Georgia. The rally attracted a crowd of some 3,000 people and undoubtedly aided in further recruiting.

Reports from federal sources and otherwise suggested Klan membership had grown to a level of 12,000 to 15,000 members by the fall of 1958. But for the most part Klan activities were confined at the time to Georgia and immediately surrounding areas. Gradually incidents of Klan-related violence began to be reported in local newspapers, seldom did they attract national attention. Edwards died in 1960, and as it had done so many times before the Klan seemed to come apart into various poorly organized factions. One of the fraction groups came under the leadership of Alabama salesman Robert Marvin Shelton. Among his friends this 'new' Imperial Wizard was fondly called Bobby. Shelton's Klan would eventually grow into one of the most violent and notorious terrorist groups of the 1960s. However Shelton's rise to power quietly began around 1961 with a series of mergers of various Klan groups including the United Klans, Knights of the Ku Klux Klan of America, and the Alabama Knights. After a series of merger meetings Shelton appeared to be in charge. In 1963 Shelton led a rally of the newly organized United Klans of America held in Tuscaloosa, Alabama. Appearing with Shelton was assistant Eugene Thomas who would become the Imperial Wizard's Exalted Cyclops. Immediately following the rally Thomas and several other Klansmen were arrested on charges of carrying concealed weapons.

By the following year the Federal Bureau of Investigation had secured informants within the United Klans of America group and was regularly receiving information on their leadership including Shelton and Thomas. One account said Thomas had warned Shelton that the Wizard may be in danger if he continued to speak out against one particular Klan splinter group. In addition to other things the Shelton-led Klan was also stockpiling weapons. Under Shelton and Thomas the issue was not so much protection as it was aggression. In September of 1964 after a UKA rally, Thomas led a group of fellow Klansmen to a nightspot known as the Flame Club in

Robert M. Reed

Fairfield, Alabama. Shelton, Thomas and the others had heard rumors that both blacks and whites socialized in the club and were in fact intermingling. After some personal observations late that night Thomas expressed the necessity for the Klan to take immediate action to stamp out the "racial mixing" which he and other Klansmen had now observed. Stopping at a nearby telephone booth Thomas placed a call to an unknown source asking for dynamite, automatic weapons and hand grenades. Within less than 30 minutes Thomas and the other Klansmen were met in a secluded location by the unidentified person who had responded to the Klan phone call. To Thomas the person slipped one Thompson submachine gun, five or six grenades, and eight sticks of dynamite. Thomas and the other Klansman then drove to a secret location where they were joined by still more Klansmen. Grouped together in a number of automobiles the Klansmen drove to a public park within a few blocks of the Flame Club and waited in the darkness. FBI informants said that when police cars were noted in the area shortly afterwards the plan to bomb the club was temporarily halted.

FBI sources said the Klan group again planned the attack with dynamite one week later but this time the bombing was called off by Imperial Wizard Shelton. If the FBI knew the reasons for the abrupt change in Klan plans, confidential records released many years later make no mention of it. One memorandum did indicate however, "pertinent information concerning this matter was furnished to local law enforcement agencies and appropriate military and government agencies. But the memorandum added," the identity of the informant was not mentioned in the dissemination." Just one month later in November of 1964 the FBI confirmed that Thomas still had in his immediate possession the following:

A .38 caliber pistol, a .45 caliber pistol, an automatic shotgun, three 303 Enfield rifles, a 30-30 Winchester rifle, hand grenades, blasting caps, two M-1 rifles, a Browning automatic rifle and a German automatic pistol.

A concerned FBI took the report seriously enough to immediately dispatch the arms information to the Alcohol, Tobacco and Tax Division of the Treasury Department, the Bureau of Customs, and the United States Secret Service. Further they notified both the Civil Rights division and the Internal Security division of the United States Justice Department. Obviously the FBI at this point was not taking any chances with the likes of Shelton, Thomas and the UKA.

Night of the Klan

There is no little enemy.
—Benjamin Franklin, Poor Richard's Almanac, 1733.

Night of the Klan, A Reporter's Story

MORNING

chapter 1

They say grandfather Clarence was a Klansman back in the 1920s. While he never spoke of it, my grandmother quietly offered that sometimes people got caught up in things that were not quite what they seemed. Whatever regrets the man may have had regarding participation in such a group, such feelings were never expressed. It is doubtful that Clarence Davis, a fiery country preacher in his later years, ever came to terms with it, much less regretted it.

Here and there, in the early summer of 1967, there was talk that the Ku Klux Klan may once again be afoot in the Midwest. For the most part it was only talk. A whispered conversation in a local bar, comments at the police station, a joke at a political meeting. At the daily newspaper where I worked in Franklin, Indiana the attitude was pretty much to ignore it and perhaps it and whatever might be connected with it, would likely go away. The argument among much of the news media at the time, although not formally stated, was generally that public attention paid to such hate groups would merely give substance to any fumbling attempts these few nuts may make to be taken seriously.

Just a year earlier David Curtis Stephenson had quietly died not so far away in another Indiana community with surprisingly little coverage of his passing. As Indiana Klan chieftain during the 1920s, D.C. Stephenson had practically ruled the state while commanding thousands of followers. Eventually, after the brutal death of a young woman, Stephenson ended up in the state prison at Michigan City. By the time of his parole in the middle 1950s the Klan in Indiana was only a distant memory in the Hoosier state, if even that. As a youngster growing up in Franklin I often played in a field near Franklin High School which, as legend had it, was from time to time the site of Klan rallies and cross burnings during the 1920s. To a child it was a vast open lot used for pickup baseball and football games. I could not imagine it teeming with hundreds of robed Klansmen as older residents had, in hushed tones, sometimes described it.

All this was brought to mind one early June morning when I found a crisp, new Ku Klux Klan handbill on my office desk.

"Free Our Land, Join The Klan," it declared.

There was a drawing of a robed Klansman atop a rearing horse. Beneath it was the message that those wishing to join the Klan could write a post

Robert M. Reed

office box in Greenwood, Indiana. The name below the message was William Chaney, state coordinator for the Imperial Wizard.

Now here, in my reporter's mind, was a story of sorts. Greenwood—just to the immediate south of Indianapolis- was part of Johnson County. And Johnson County was the center of our coverage area. If Greenwood were the center for recruiting some sort of new Klan, it would make some interesting reading. As it turned out William Chaney wasn't all that hard to find. No person by that name was listed in the 'local' phone book, but the Indianapolis telephone directory had a couple. Picking the one with the closest location to the Greenwood city limits, I quickly dialed the number.

A man answered and confirmed he was Bill Chaney.

"Are you the one with the post office box for the Klan?", I asked quickly.

"Yes, are you interested in join'in up?"

No, I explained, I was a newspaper reporter looking for some information. He seemed a bit disappointed, but still willing to talk. Chaney confirmed for me that the post office box had been in operation for a few months and further that he was the state coordinator for the project. (Later I would learn that the national United Klans of America appointed 'representatives' to state regions where membership was undeveloped. Once the membership number rose, the Klansman was rewarded with the new rank of Grand Dragon.)

"So is there an active Klan here?"

Chaney was being careful by now, "I can't comment on that at the present time. But if there isn't one formed already in these areas, we will take steps to establish one."

He admitted that there were some regularly scheduled meetings of Klan members in various parts of Indiana, and elsewhere "we are quietly building." Chaney added that Klan meetings were normally closed to the public, but there were plans for a major public rally in the future. "We are attending to things," he concluded with a soft drawl.

Sixty seconds after the conversation I was on the telephone to the Indianapolis bureau of the Federal Bureau of Investigation.

An agent returned my call about 15 minutes later. (At the time the FBI almost always insisted on reporters leaving their phone number so it could be confirmed as a legitimate news agency.) When the agent admitted that the bureau was indeed investigating the Klan in the Indiana area the confirmation came as a mild surprise. Typically the FBI would say no comment and just as typically the news story would simply report they were contacted but declined talk. However my willing FBI source was not going beyond the basic confirmation. Any thing else would be "too specific" I was told. Fair enough. A decent story anyway.

Night of the Klan, A Reporter's Story

The story on the Klan's membership campaign via a Greenwood post office box appeared in June 8, 1967. It attracted little attention. People had read about the 'new' Klan a few previous times in the middle 1960s. Rallies had been scheduled in 1964 and 1965 on farms near Greenfield and Lawrenceburg but both had been either broken up by police or outlawed by city officials before they could happen. In 1965 the highest ranking leader of the United Klans of America, Imperial Wizard Robert Shelton had visited Greenfield at least once in an attempt to persuade city officials to allow a KKK rally there. City officials there rejected the idea and Shelton's mission failed.

Just a week after the Journal story on the latest Klan effort broke, representative Chaney telephoned me at the newspaper office. He wanted to know if we could get together "for a little chat. I might have a story for ya too."

That same afternoon I got my first face-to-face look at Chaney who now introduced himself as the Grand Dragon of the Indiana Ku Klux Klan. He was neatly dressed in suit and tie, clutching a dapper straw hat. Large and balding, he wore a large Masonic ring on his hand and spoke with a slight drawl that native Hoosiers would have recognized as being somewhere from neighboring Kentucky. Turns out he was a native of Somerset, Kentucky, and served in the military, and now was very much interested in promoting the Klan. In his own polite way he quietly explained that the Klan was definitely opposed to communism, hoped to re-establish constitutional government in America, maintain racial purity, and restore white supremacy. For good measure, he also threw in that the Klan was fully opposed to the United Nations and believed devoutly in "America for Americans."

As far as the news he offered to bring, Chaney said there would be a very public appearance by the Klan in the near future and that it would involved a number of Indiana towns. He would let me know as the details became available. After that the Grand Dragon, always neat appearing and usually wearing a side arm beneath his jacket made regular visits to the Journal newsroom.(I assumed he had a valid license to carry a firearm but it never came up during those early conversations. Ultimately I would be summoned before a Grand Jury to tell what I knew about Chaney and the weapons he carried.) Chaney never came alone. Sometimes he would bring along a fellow Klan member with some official-sounding title. At other times he would simply explain that the person with him then was his "security" officer.

It was during one of these frequent visits that Chaney disclosed the Klan would be going public with a motorcade to Greenwood, Whiteland, Franklin, Bargersville, Mooresville, and Martinsville. Others were working

Robert M. Reed

out the details, he said, but the Klan chief was sure it would open up some eyes. As it happen on a bright Saturday in late July it did open some eyes. There were dozens of vehicles in the Klan motorcade that day, and they were filled with robed members of the Ku Klux Klan. Throughout the communities just south of Indianapolis it was an amazing sight. It was as the newspaper later reported the first Main Street view of the Klan in nearly 40 years, "and probably won't be the last."

The strange motorcade drove around the Johnson County courthouse in Franklin around 1 p.m. after first forming on Fry Road near Greenwood shortly after noon and driving down US 31 through New Whiteland and Whiteland. Leading the way was a pick-up truck with a hand-painted sign proclaiming, "Fight communism, back our boys in Vietnam, from the Morgan county Klan." By-standers watched with little comment as the 'Klan caravan' drove the main highways from community to community with American and Confederate flags waving in the mid-day sun. They're only stop that day was in downtown Martinsville. Chaney in a striking green robe instead of his usual dapper street clothes led the group, which included an assortment of rank-denoting robes of various colors.

Local and state police, alerted ahead of time, flanked the downtown streets in impressive numbers. "There will be no trouble unless the Klan starts it," Martinsville police chief Jack Stanley assured reporters. When an argument broke out between a Klan member distributing literature and a patron who had just stepped out of the local tavern, police interceded. The patron who undoubtedly was very surprised to find the once quite streets filled with Klansmen, was promptly arrested for public intoxication.

Along one Martinsville street a group of teenagers were carrying their own home-made sign. It read, "stop this madness-Go Home KKK."

EARLY AFTERNOON

chapter 2

In fact the 'madness' was only beginning.

On Monday afternoon following the Saturday of KKK activities the Daily Journal's front page was heavy with race-related news stories. In Detroit, Michigan governor George Romney had announced that President Johnson had granted his appeal to send 5,000 federal troops "into Detroit to help battle the Negro rioting which has spread death, arson and looting though wide stretches of the city." Five persons were reported dead and some 800 injured. In Newark, New Jersey meanwhile, the first national conference of black power had ended with approval of resolutions calling for revolutionary action to end "black bondage" in America. The daily newspaper in Franklin also carried a page one story regarding the local Klan event, along with pictures that showed Chaney in his glimmering Grand Dragon uniform talking to citizens in the downtown area of neighboring Martinsville. The tone of the Klan story was that while many watched few were moved. A woman in Greenwood told a reporter afterwards, "the Klan got about as much recognition as a funeral procession when they went through here." In Franklin, police officer Dale Furrer confirmed, "people around here just weren't interested."

However Chaney and those in the higher-ranking levels of the United Klans of America considered the public motorcade to be a good first step. Ten days later they announced plans for a major rally in northern Johnson County. This time the event would involve the burning of a 75-foot cross. Selected for the rally site was a farm field five miles south of Glen's Valley, it was then basically a fairly isolated location near State Road 37 at a point between Mooresville and Greenwood. Indiana's new Grand Dragon boasted the rally would attract 1,000 to 2,500 people and would extend from afternoon to late evening. Chaney further assured the burning of the giant cross on a nearby hilltop, a traditional final act of Klan rallies, "will be visible for miles."

Chaney related to me and other news media at the time that the rally was being expressly designed to "acquaint white Americans with the United Klans of America and to rededicate ourselves to our unfinished work." Apparently their unfinished work also involved bringing in various Grand Dragons from other states, national Klan leaders, and the number-one Klan commander in the United States, Imperial Wizard of the United Klans of America one Robert Shelton. During the previous two years Shelton, son of a Tuscaloosa grocer and himself a former tire factory worker had advanced the Klan membership in Alabama to more than twice what it had been. Among some ten rival Klan groups vying for membership in the South, Shelton had built the United Klans of America into the largest organization of them all. He had begun mainly by strong recruiting in counties and communities surrounding industrial Birmingham. Eventually, according to some estimates, Shelton's organization had established units in over 100 counties (or Klaverns) in a seven state area. It was not too difficult to visualize that Shelton and the Klan leaders had a similar development plan for the outer regions of industrial Indianapolis and other parts of the Midwest.

Just a year earlier the Attorney General of Alabama, Richmond Flowers had disclosed an investigation showing that Shelton's Klan now "wields a frightening influence in Alabama. It resembles a shadow government, making its own laws, manipulating local politics, burrowing into some of our local law enforcements."

"The average Kluxer is a fifth-grade school dropout, with a background of social and economic failure," Flowers had observed the summer before. "Because he cannot qualify for the future, he fights it. In doing so, he drives away the quality industries that could come in and lift him out of the squalor."

And while some deadly crimes certainly bore the 'shadow' of the Klan, there were no major matching criminal convictions as yet to prove it to the nation.

In September of 1963 three Ku Klux Klan members were immediately arrested after the bombing of the Sixteenth Street Baptist Church in Birmingham. The tragic bombing had killed four black children who were waiting in the church basement for Sunday morning services. Apparently the bomb had been planted behind the church steps on the Saturday night before the services. At 10:19 a.m. it exploded killing Addie Mae Collins, Carole Robertson, Cynthia Wesley and Denise McNair. The first three victims were age 14, while Denise McNair was 11-years-old.

The Klansmen were members of the same KKK organization and had been further connected with the possession of illegal explosives. After being held in jail they were eventually charged only with the illegal possession of dynamite. In a secret memorandum sent to Federal Bureau of Investigation director J. Edgar Hoover, field agents flatly stated, "the bombing was the handiwork of Klansman Robert E. Cambliss, Bobby Frank Cherry, Herman Frank Cash and Thomas E. Blanton, Jr." Despite the memorandum and other information no further action was taken. This relatively minor conviction, on possession of explosives, eventually was overturned by a higher court and the Klansmen were freed. Many years later documents from the United States Justice Department revealed that Hoover had deliberately blocked the prosecution of the Klan members at the time. In doing so the FBI director had rejected recommendations of FBI agents that testimony identifying the suspects be forwarded to federal prosecutors. Apparently Hoover felt that too much attention directed toward the Klan and its terrorist activities in the 1960s might further enhance and inspire the Civil Rights movement, which he believed was suspect. By the summer of 1967 (- as the Klan sought to make inroads in the Midwest -) as far as federal authorities were concerned the church bombing and the resulting deaths in the south were totally unsolved and very near to being officially closed.

Less than a year after the Birmingham church bombing, three civil rights workers were murdered in Mississippi. This time however Imperial Wizard Shelton had turned from a dark silence to defiant denials on the part of the Klan. As the grim search for the three victims was underway, Shelton told the news media from his Klan headquarters that the disappearance of the three was merely a hoax.

"These people like to dramatize situations in order to milk the public of more money for their causes. They hope to raise two hundred and fifty thousand dollars for their campaign in Mississippi, and I understand these funds are slow coming in. So create a hoax like this, put weeping mothers and wives on national television, and try to touch the hearts of the nation. Their whole purpose is just to get more money."

However Shelton was again silent when the bodies were finally discovered, hidden in a remote area of that state. Six members of the White Knights of the Klu Klux Klan were among those arrested and charged with the federal crime of conspiring to violate the civil and constitutional rights of the three murder victims. In the summer of 1967 they were still months away from trial on federal charges. No state murder charges had been filed against any of the group.

In 1965 a black military officer Lt. Colonel Lemuel Penn left Ft. Benning, Georgia driving home to Washington, D.C where, in civilian life, he was an educator. As Col. Penn and two passengers drove a lonely stretch of highway, their vehicle was overtaken by a car containing three male occupants. The blast from two shotguns killed Penn instantly. The two passengers escaped serious injury. After three weeks of intensive investigation, the FBI arrested three Klansmen who were all members of the Clark County Klavern 244 of the United Klans of America. They carried membership cards signed by Imperial Wizard Shelton. One of the three, James Lackey, finally confessed to driving the car from which the deadly gun blasts came. One Klansman with him fired one shotgun he said, and a second Klansman fired another shotgun. In 1966 the two alleged KKK gunmen were convicted in federal court and given ten- year sentences for conspiring to violate the rights of officer Penn. At that time Shelton had no comment.

Moreover authorities were at some point of the opinion that Shelton was himself connected directly to much of the headlined violence. They would eventually learn of Shelton's leadership in a super-secret Klan elite group known as Nacirema. (American spelled backwards.) During the 1960s this select group reportedly trained for what federal investigators would term "more violent action" in the Klan fight against blacks and the Civil Rights Movement. While Shelton was busily making visits to the Midwest in the latter 1960s he was, according to one federal investigator's later Congressional testimony, also busy directing "an organization of back-robed Klansmen suspected of participating in racial bombings" at various locations.

Back in Johnson County, Indiana in early August of 1967, Johnson County prosecutor Joe VanValer was not taking a chance on the newly active Klan gaining inroads right in his own backyard. On August 7, 1967 the prosecutor file a motion in Johnson Superior court asking for a temporary restraining order banning the state-wide rally scheduled for the following Saturday. Two days later Superior Court Judge Jack Rogers issued that restraining order. Further, he directed Grand Dragon Chaney to appear the following Monday for a hearing on making the order permanent. VanValer had acted on the terms of Indiana's 1947 Anti-Hate Law, which had been used just two years earlier in 1965 to prevent a different Klan group for holding a rally in Indiana's Dearborn County (near Lawrenceburg, Indiana). In keeping with that law, the temporary order barred, "confederating, associating or assembling at any time in Johnson County for the purpose of advocating or disseminating malicious hatred by reason of race, color or religion."

Chaney, up until then a fairly smooth and self-assuming Klan spokesman seemed to be caught a bit off guard by prosecutor VanValer's dramatic action.

"This is infringing on our constitutional rights. It will be tested. As far as I am concerned we will rally anyway," he related on the telephone to me. But then quickly added, "that is, if it is left up to me."

As it turns out the court challenge to the Indiana Klan's march to membership would not be left up to Chaney. Klan attorneys immediately filed a counter-plea in Johnson Superior Court to dismiss the injunction. The temporary injunction remained thus blocking the Saturday KKK rally but setting the stage for a legal battle on the larger issue. Just to be on the safe side, in light of Chaney's threat earlier to hold the rally anyway, VanValer rode in an Indiana Police helicopter over the planned site that particular

Saturday morning. There was no sign of a 75-foot cross or anything else in the empty field.

Chaney's "plea in abatement" had asked Judge Rogers to dismiss the prosecutor's petition. Among other things it maintained that the Johnson County court had no jurisdiction because Grand Dragon Chaney was a resident of Marion County and Imperial Wizard Robert Shelton, who had also been named in the prosecutor's petition, was a resident of Alabama. Still it was also apparently the signal for Imperial Wizard Shelton to finally make an appearance on the embattled scene.

In mid-August the Klan's highly regarded Shelton arrived at Weir Cook airport in Indianapolis where, appearing with Chaney by his side, he told reporters the Klan would use all legal means to fight the restraining order and then reschedule the long pending rally. Shelton and Chaney then climbed into a car and drove directly to a Greenwood restaurant where I had been invited to meet the Imperial Wizard in person.

Unlike the large-figured and often smiling Chaney, Shelton was by contrast slightly built, thin-faced and grim. Some years later best-selling author Donald Whitehead would describe the Shelton of that era as "a lean, brooding man with deepest eyes and a fanatic's zeal for his mission of returning the Klan to its former position of power." Shelton began his Klan operations with the Alabama Knights of the Klu Klux Klan. Gradually he became more powerful and formed the United Klans of America. It was UKA that eventually reached out to appoint Chaney in Indiana. In 1965 the Imperial Wizard had been hauled before the House Committee on Un-American Activities to testify about some of the Klan-related terrorists acts that had occurred in the South. Shelton took the Fifth Amendment, refusing to provide much information beyond his name, age, and place of birth. One summer night during the early 1960s, Shelton addressed a Klan rally in Mississippi that drew 800 followers. The following summer, at similar location the Imperial Wizard's 'klanvocation' drew several thousand Klan members and sympathizers. His influence was clearly growing in the South and elsewhere.

The Imperial Wizard did not often talk to the news media, and when he did Shelton was careful to present his Klan as misunderstood patriots. Of course, "only white, gentile, Protestant, native-born Americans can take the Klan oath, since the Knights of the Ku Klux Klan is a fraternal order of real men who are 100-percent American. But the Jew or Catholic might be welcomed into the Klan if he qualified." Moreover the Wizard told at least one interviewer that while the Klan did burn crosses, it was simply "to show the light of truth to the world. We use it to rally Christians and to meet the oncoming tide of Communism. The organization doesn't participate in burning crosses of intimidation. When we have a problem to discuss with any individual, a committee of one, two or three Klansmen in street clothes will approach this person to discuss any grievances we may have with him, to give him our point of view, to persuade him to see things our way."

Immediately after Shelton's refusal to testify in any real detail before the House Committee on Un-American Activities, the Wizard told reporters he was acting to protect his sacred oath by not divulging "Klan secrets." Besides he was opposed to the Congressional investigation because it was based merely on FBI misinformation. "The FBI has already slandered the Klan by calling it a subversive organization, which is an outrageous lie." On the other hand he did allow that other Klan groups aside from the United Klans of America could be indeed subversive. Shelton added the comment in a national magazine interview, "there are several Klans you know. That is the trouble of throwing every nut in the same bag and saying it's all the same kind of nuts."

Nuts or not, the Federal Bureau of Investigation had been watching the Imperial Wizard very closely during that period of time. Confidential documents, made available through research many years later, showed Shelton's name linked to the investigation of numerous acts of violence. Informants regularly told of Shelton's contact with Klansman known to have committed criminal acts including bombings and shootings. It was clear that Imperial Wizard Robert "Bobby" Shelton was their leader.

We sat face to face at the table that same day in Greenwood. Two of Shelton's bodyguards sat at a table nearby. All were neatly dressed in business suits and red ties. (A long time later I would learn that the significance of the red ties was to alert other Klan members to the fact they were indeed personal armed guards of the Wizard.)

"So you're the reporter around here," Shelton said to me making it seem more like a statement than a question.

Shelton did not wait for a reply nor did his face show any real emotion.

"I'm Bobby Shelton, Imperial Wizard of United Klans of America," he added.

Mr. Wizard then went right to the point.

"You know I think that prosecutor you have around here is a real dictator," he said flatly. "Maybe you ought to get together and have him fired or something."

I explained that prosecutor VanValer had been elected by a large majority and was pretty popular with people in Johnson County.

Shelton went right on, saying he considered this particular county to be a "police state…, which is denying the rights of free speech and free assembly."

"Well they consider your Klan to be a hate group," I said.

Night of the Klan, A Reporter's Story

The Imperial Wizard took a breath, and seemed more than a little annoyed by the reference.

"We're making no cries of hatred here," he said. "As a matter of fact, I am confused as to the definition of hatred in Indiana."

If this was supposed to be an opportunity to explain the term hatred to the most powerful KKK leader in the nation as we sat quietly over cooling hamburgers and fries, I decided it would be a wasted one.

Even then, at that time and place, Shelton readily acknowledged he and his cohorts were being watch both from out and from within by the FBI. "All they have to do is fill out an application, and we will welcome them into the Klan and have fraternal unionism. It's not necessary for them to infiltrate. They have informers who are actually turning the money they get for informing to the FBI back to the Klan itself. We play their game. We move on to other things."

The Wizard sat silent for the moment, and adjusted his black knit tie and his jacket. He briefly glanced at the Klan guard to his right, looked around the room, and raised his hand in a sweeping gesture. The little finger on one hand sparkled with a large diamond ring. He again faced me without showing any expression, not waiting for questions.

Without hesitation Shelton went on to condemn the civil rights movement as being "composed of sex perverts, beatniks, pinkos, Communists, and the lowest misfits from all over the country." Further he made reference, as he had to others, of "counter-agents working with the federal government who have signed notarized statements saying there are many active Communists in the civil rights struggle." The Klan on the other hand, continued Shelton, was there to provide power to white Americans "only the pure race has the highest degree of ability to govern. The Klan has its mission, and it is not the same of the Reconstruction era. This is not the Klan of our forefathers, because this is a different time."

The Wizard too another hurried look around the dining area., and made a faint smile.

"You are the local reporter," he said quietly. "The local reporter like you is alright, trying to make a living for his family. It is the editorial head offices that you find the distortion directed by this conspiratorially controlled press. The national news media creates anything that is sensational, that will sell copy. They go out of their way to grasp anything that appears sensational in racial demonstrations to sell news. We expect more from you."

Then the interview was over. Shelton was up on his feet looking about. Grand Dragon Chaney was standing as well. The Klan entourage, lead by the two guards, left hurriedly once the meal was completed. Shelton was ushered into the back seat of a black Cadillac in the parking lot, and the vehicle with its small Confederate flag flapping from its windshield mount rushed onto U.S. 31. From Greenwood, Shelton and his guards were headed to the Louisville, Kentucky area in general and the small suburban community of Middletown.

At Middletown Klan chieftains had hoped to conduct a greater Louisville rally similar to what they had hoped to be a greater Indianapolis rally near Greenwood. Shelton and the Klan ultimately struck out there too.

A Jefferson (Ky.) Country ruled in favor of an injunction declaring the scene of the rally would be a "disruptive and irreparable injury and harm would result to the people." The judge warned further that any such demonstrations "deprived citizens of their right to peace, calm and tranquility." The judge observed that even the cross burning was illegal in the state of Kentucky. As a result Shelton, and Klan representatives from Kentucky, Ohio, Indiana and anywhere else had nowhere to go.

Despite the injunction, several carloads of Klansmen approached the rally site where a Jefferson county law enforcement police officer stopped them at an intersection and read them the court order. The Klansmen left without further incident.

Back in Indiana, prosecutor VanValer's efforts to obtain a permanent injunction against Klan rallies in Johnson County had been delayed indefinitely. Earlier in the Dearborn County case of 1965, prosecutor Harry Zerbe had first obtained a temporary order restraining a Klan rally near Dillsboro, and then dismissed his own petition for a permanent injunction before a hearing could be held. Zerbe's thinking had apparently been that with the order dismissed the Klan would have no legal recourse in seeking to test the 1947 anti-hate law. A permanent injunction however could have been subject to Klan appeal.

VanValer seemed more than willing to stand by the anti-hate law throughout the legal process. The Klan organization's reasoning appeared to be that it might be simpler and less costly to just seek another site for any future rallies.

By early mid-September Grand Dragon Chaney had backed away considerably from the idea of holding a KKK rally in Johnson County. While he still hoped to return to the original rally site at Glen's Valley, he said "legal proceedings" in Johnson Superior Court made it doubtful.

Never-the-less Chaney vowed to hold a statewide rally, complete with cross burning somewhere in Indiana before November 1. The Grand Dragon added further than charters had been granted for Ku Klux Klan united in Johnson and Grant counties. Units, he said, were then operating from post office boxes in Whiteland and Marion, Indiana. By the middle of October in 1967 at any idea of a public and massive Klan rally in Indiana seem to have been put aside by Chaney and the other Klan leaders. Instead they announced plans for a 500-mile motorcade by the end of the month. The idea was to more or less to form a symbolic cross within the boundaries of the state.

Chaney told the news media that on a Saturday the first motorcade would drive along US 40 from the Ohio state line westward through Richmond, Knightstown, Greenfield, Indianapolis, Plainfield, and Terre Haute. On the following Sunday the Klan motorcade would drive US 31 from the Michigan line north of South Bend southward through Plymouth, Kokomo, Carmel, Indianapolis, Greenwood, Whiteland, Franklin, Columbus, and Jeffersonville.

The cross-like route, according to Chaney, was designed to "be symbolic of the Old Rugged Cross." According to Klan tradition the hymn, The Old Rugged Cross, was sung during burning of the cross at the conclusion of KKK rallies. The Grand Dragon added however that there were to be no rallies or gatherings in connection with the motorcade in any of the cities and town they would be passing through. Ohio Klansmen were to be part of the first motorcade, and many of them would also drive to the South Bend areas the following day to ride in the second motorcade trip. "The purpose is to inform the public that the Klan is still active and alive in Indiana and many other states," Chaney added.

It too attracted little attention. Moreover, it would be the last really public activity for the Klan in Indiana for sometime. After that most of their events were generally by invitation only. Chaney never mentioned the lackluster 'Crossing' in the weeks that followed. He did however, seem anxious to 'visit' either by telephone calls to my office or directly by stopping by the Daily Journal building in Franklin.

Now that Chaney was the certified Grand Dragon of the Indiana Klu Klux Klan he never came by the office alone. Always there was one other Klansman. Sometimes he brought along a Klansman said to be an official of the group in Michigan, Ohio or some other area. At other times it was a security guard, or a ranking officer from one of the surrounding counties or Klaverns. For a time one of Chaney's regulars was the Exalted Cylops Donald Haymaker who claimed to be in charge of several nearby counties. If you examined these visitors closely enough you might notice a lapel pin indicating their membership in the Klan. But generally there was nothing in their outward appearance to draw unwarranted attention to them.

If I wasn't on deadline at the daily newspaper, we would sit in the newspaper's small conference room and sip ill-tasting vending machine coffee while Chaney would update the Klan's recruiting activities around Indiana and surrounding states. None of the information appeared to be newsworthy, but, taken all together I figured it somehow might be helpful later. After each visit I would usually make a few notes for my Klan file, but as far as news coverage was concerned the Klan had temporarily put aside public events and was clearly taking a different direction. My guess was that it may have been because recruiting was doing well and they didn't need any undue attention at this point from the media. Or perhaps the earlier failed attempts at massive public rallies had been a bit embarrassing. At any rate I was soon going to get a much closer look.

On a chilly November afternoon in 1967, Grand Dragon Chaney telephoned me once again at the office.

"Would you be interested," Chaney asked finally, "if I arranged it so you could attend one of our meetings?"

"You mean a Klan rally?"

"No," Chaney continued. "These are sort of... business meetings. You would be our guest. They are sort of., well, not open to the public, you know."

"Well, sure," I responded, but yet wondering really if it was such a good idea. Meeting these Klan characters in the newspaper office was one thing. But closed meetings, some other place were another matte

"Okay, that's fine," Chaney approved. He carefully detailed the time and location of the meeting. It was to be held upstairs above a private fraternal organization bar on the south side of Indianapolis.

"Tell the bartender you're there for a meeting," he said much more quietly on the phone. Then he added, "Ask for the Kennel Club."

LATE AFTERNOON

chapter 3

Claudette, my wife, was extremely opposed to me attending any secret meetings of the Ku Klux Klan even if they chose to call themselves the Kennel Club. Especially, if these strange people referred to themselves as the so-called Kennel Club.

"This just isn't right," she warned me as soon as the few details slipped from my mouth.

"Why the dog business?", she questioned. "Why are they hiding around?"

I couldn't think of any especially good reason.

Claudette and I had been high school sweethearts. Our romance had developed through the giddy but gritty days of drive-ins and junior proms and kept right on growing. It defied the cultural experts who have spent the past half century explaining that high school romances were the cotton-candy of life and just about as enduring as a carnival ride. The two of us had grown up in the same small town and enjoyed the simple life it offered. After I had graduated from Franklin High School I enrolled in Franklin College as a journalism major while Claudette, three years younger, completed high school. Three months after her graduation from FHS we were married.

During my college days I worked as many hours as possible for the Johnson County News, a thriving weekly newspaper based in Greenwood. Mostly I covered county government at the Johnson County courthouse and just about every law enforcement agency in the county. Just as soon as I obtained my journalism degree, another newspaper opportunity arose. Home News Enterprises, publishers of the Columbus Republican in Columbus, had decided to launch a entirely new newspaper in Johnson County. The plan was to construct a new building and go head-to-head with the established Franklin newspaper, The Evening Star. It sounded like fun, so I signed up.

By the middle November of 1967 the 'high school sweethearts' had added two children to their family. Matthew was not much more than a year old, and Judith was about three and a half years old.

"You know you have two little children to think of as well," Claudette reminded me very pointedly as conversation on Klan matters ended. "The newspaper doesn't own you. We do."

But her little hug told me it was okay, at least for now, to see what the Klan was all about.

39

Robert M. Reed

Carefully aware of her admonishment, and her love, I made the trip to my first 'non public' meeting. The fraternal club bar was not too difficult to locate even in the dark November evening. Inside a country-western tune was playing softly as I approached the bar. Luckily there were few patrons that Wednesday evening. I felt a little stupid approaching the bartender and asking about a meeting upstairs as if I was an actor in some sort of spy movie.

"I'm here for a meeting," I said. Then probably too quickly added, "It's the Kennel Club."

"Upstairs," he said pointing upward with glass he had been wiping.

Actually it turned out to be the third floor. I followed a few notes tacked to the walls of the hallway until I came door with the light from inside shining through. Opening the door I gazed upon about two dozen folding chairs lined up in small rows and six or eight men milling about. Chaney, in a business suit, immediately greeted me and began introducing me to various individuals and Klan officials. Presently others arrived until the room was about two-thirds full. All wore street clothes, with not a robe in sight.

Chaney called upon the Kludd for a prayer. The Kludd turned out to be term for the Klan group's chaplain. An older, gray-haired man appeared and offered a brief prayer. Then Chaney asked everyone to be seated and the Ku Klux Klan meeting began. To be totally honest, the meeting part of it at that stage was not a lot different than any other social-club kind of session with reports, future events, and the mention of dues.

I was largely ignored until I slipped my notebook out of my jacket and began idly taking notes.

"Mr. Reed, you can't do that," said a firm voice behind me.

I turned to face a husky man with a wary smile. I had never seen him before, but he apparently knew me.

"Mr. Chaney asked that no notes be taken," he said and then repeated, "so you can't do that."

I returned the notebook to my jacket, making a point to never repeat the same mistake. From that point on, through numerous 'non-public' meetings I took notes only after I had left the group and was safely out of sight in my car. Then I jotted down all the details of what occurred that evening. When the business meeting had ended Chaney was there politely thanking me for attending and telling me there would be other meetings in the months ahead.

"You might want to bring your camera along the next time," said. "Our security guards will be there then in their uniforms."

The next time following instructions, I brought my camera but left my trusty notebook in the car. True to his word the Grand Dragon had four uniformed security guards in attendance at my second 'business' meeting of the Klan. Unlike the street clothes of all the others at the meeting, the chosen costume of these security guards would have attracted attention on just about any street corner in America. They wore white helmet liners emblazoned with an Klan cross enclosed in a circle. They wore a similar symbolic patch on the shoulder of their uniform shirts. They also wore shoulder lanyards. Two of the four wore ties with a Klan emblem affixed to them. Each had a white belt with a brass buckle. The four security guards had no weapons of any kind in sight. I was later told however that at most meetings the outer guard—-usually two of the four—were always armed, and that many of the Klansmen themselves usually came armed.

Chaney encouraged me photograph the Klan guards as the meeting concluded, and I did. He warned me against photographing other members, and I did not.

"These guards," Chaney told me, were merely doorkeepers such as any lodge or fraternal group would have. Over the many months that followed I would learn that in fact the security guards were actually there to maintain order and to protect their Grand Dragon leader at all costs. When the Indiana Klan again began making public appearances, the security guard was always present, and consequently they were eventually regularly photographed by newspaper photographers and other interested parties.

There were other revelations too. The Kennel Club connection, for example, was a play on the Klan password called CA BARK. It meant Constantly Applied By All Real Klansmen. The password CLASP was similar, in connotation, Clannish Loyalty A Sacred Principle. As Grand Dragon, Chaney reigned over what in Klan terms was a Realm that was more or less a given state such as Indiana. Meanwhile the 'Invisible Empire, to which each Klan member swore an allegiance, had no real boundaries. They considered it to be everywhere. Joining meant they took their oath to the Invisible Empire of the Klan and left behind all else. "All things and matters which do not exist within this Order or are not authorized by or do not come under its jurisdiction shall be designated as the Alien World," said their secret creed. "All persons who are not members shall be designated as Alien."

Despite an occasional invitation to a meeting, or increasingly frequent visits to the newspaper, I was always regarded as an alien by the KKK, however I was one alien they were willing to communicate with in an effort to present their case to the public.

The Klan was clearly hungry for membership.

"We are planting the seed in the Midwest and the Far West," a representative of one national Klan organization told a national magazine. "They are crying for us outside the South and we are answering the call." Besides Indiana, there were reports among Klan watchers at the time that recruiting was about to become active in West Virginia, Minnesota, Iowa, Pennsylvania, Wisconsin and California. Chaney regularly made reference to friendly Klan groups in Michigan and Ohio.

Some accounts credited the various Klan organizations of the latter 1960s with having enrolled in excess of 40,000 members mostly from the South and Midwest. Although Klan officials tended to inflate their membership figures both locally and nationally, law enforcement officials were almost just as inclined to go the other way and under estimate them. While Klan membership late in that 1960s decade were a far cry from the millions said to have been enrolled during the 1920s, they were by most anyone's count much higher than they had ever been since the Roaring Twenties. And it was not just a matter of number. An investigative report published in the Saturday Evening Post in 1965 noted the 'new' Klan of Shelton and Chaney and the rest was "potentially more dangerous than the old Klan of the 1920s." Leaders of the 'new' Klan "at not interested primarily in the money, but are grimly dedicated men determined to maintain white supremacy at whatever cost."

Of course not just anyone would do for Klan membership either. The potential member had to be native-born, Gentile person, and be not only white but willing to "faithfully strive for the eternal maintenance of white supremacy." A membership application blank urged "join today if you are against Communist inspired race mixing, if your are a true patriot."

"You know what happens when a superior race mixes with an inferior one," Chaney told his audiences. "The civilization sinks to the lower level of the inferior race. It happened in Egypt and it happened in India, and we don't want it to happen here."

Annual dues for Klan membership were $12 payable upon joining. Members were also charged an additional "naturalization" fee of $15 to become a full citizen of the Invisible Empire. Such an organization would not appeal to the majority of people, and the Klan knew it. They were quite content to 'reach out' to those who felt threatened.

During the 1960s, journalists James Batten and Dwayne Walls had observed in the Charlotte (North Carolina) Observer that typically Klan members were "the backwash of white society, the low-income, poorly educated farmer or laborer who sees in the Ku Klux Klan the only champion of his cause and the only hope of preserving his station in society's changing order." Meanwhile the Saturday Evening Post's investigative report had concluded that taken over all the Klan at that point was "less an organization than the manifestation of a state of mind-the despair of the poor white in a society in which he can find no respected place."

Chaney, in my observations at the time, fit the description well.

Night of the Klan, A Reporter's Story

"Actually I've been a Klansman all my life and didn't know it," Chaney frequently explained regarding his own personal involvement in the Klan. He maintained he had been influenced into being a part of the Klan when, as a small boy, he saw his grandfather's participation in such a group first in Illinois, and again later in Kentucky.

When pressed a bit more Chaney said his individual connection with the United Klans of America began around 1963 or 1964 in Greenfield. He became the representative for the Indiana Realm shortly afterwards, serving under the immediate direction of Robert Shelton. Chaney referred to some others organizing events in Hancock, Morgan and Owen counties but was purposefully vague on the details and also sparse on what further role Shelton played in the Klan's regional recruiting efforts. Chaney's involvement in the Klan throughout that period was pretty much full-time although he did apparently work at various part-time jobs in the Indianapolis area to provide additional income. At one time he was employed by a motorcycle escort service, at another time Chaney was handling freight out of the Indianapolis airport.

On the other hand Chaney was eternally mum regarding any information dealing directly with membership of the Klan in Indiana. Not only did he repeatedly decline to provide any numbers, he was also carefully non-specific on locations of Klan klaverns around the state. From time to time he mentioned counties, but for the most part he did not. He did once claim to have two or three klaverns operating within the confines of Indianapolis. He said the details were confidential. The actual membership list was said to have been carefully guarded by Chaney himself. A Klan security guard who testified under oath for the Johnson County prosecutor's office admitted the membership list "would be a valuable piece of information for anybody to have, but nobody had it but Mr. Chaney."

"I knew some (members)", the guard answered to further questioning, "but no I didn't know all of them, of course not."

All members knew the officers however. They knew who the Exalted Cyclops was and that he directed the local klavern. Sometimes they merely referred to that officer as E.C. The Cyclops, meanwhile, had klavern staff officers also known as Terrors that included the Kalaliff or vice president, the Klokard or teacher of Klankraft, and various inner and outer guards. There was also a Klan officer designated as the Night Hawk, a Klansman in charge of the induction of members and the burning of the rally cross, among other things. It was said that the Night Hawk could even wear a black robe at rallies and during some other appearances, but I never personally saw such a black costume. Beyond the few officers, the majority of the Klan members seemed to have no major role in the organization other than to attend events and carry out orders.

Robert M. Reed

The Klan "has a use for the people it feels are less important," observed Gary Thomas Rowe Jr. in his book, My Undercover Years With The Ku Klux Klan. "They are given the dangerous work to do. Rarely are any of the brass involved in violence; they feel it is their role to create a respectable public image." Rowe, who eventually became an FBI informant and finally was a willing witness in the murder of a white civil rights worker who had offered a ride to black activist, added, "the lackeys are assigned to put up posters or carry out night raids which the officials will later publicly deny, but they are not invited to officers' meetings."

Years later, thanks in a large part to the Freedom of Information Act, I was able to connect the Federal Bureau of Investigation's very high interest in Klan activities in this region of the country. The Indiana State Police seemed to have an interest at the time but federal involvement was a mystery—at least as far as this newspaper reporter was concern. In reality very confidential FBI memorandums were making reference to the situation just as I was plodding along the inquiring reporter route. One particular memo sought to allay near constant concerns of the United States Justice Department that any wiretapping or electronic surveillance was being used to monitor the Klan's various operations. FBI sources insisted such devices probably were not in use however they confided there were "several complicated cases involving allegations of conspiracy by members of various Ku Klux Klan groups. Confidential information from various sources unknown...was used in developing the facts in several cases." The translation was apparently, given the informants they were forced to use, they could not really say with any absolute certainty how they were gathering information.

One day in the midst of all this I got a visit at the newspaper office from Indiana State Police detective Richard L. Bumps. Officer Bumps was a big, husky, tough-appearing guy who looked much more like a movie hoodlum than a law enforcement officer. It was his 'tough guy' looks and as well as his uncanny sense of what was happening at all levels of criminal developments, that would later lead him into major roles of undercover work for the Indiana State police and other law enforcement agencies. His job got to be the type of real dangerous, demanding totally alternative lifestyle work that took a tremendous toll on the cop who excelled at it. In the late 1960s Bumps was a very smart detective who seemed to know at least a little about everything going on at the time, from the drug underworld to the radical world of the Klu Klux Klan.

Over the years Bumps had proven himself to me to be a very reliable source of information. Some things he offered could be used in a current story but never with attribution. Some things he offered were strictly for background and never to be used in print. And still other things, such as the kind of information you neither used nor background. You simply forgot you ever heard it. Those were the unwritten rules. And they were never broken. Like any worthwhile newspaper reporter, I enjoyed the confidence of many quality police officers at different levels law enforcement. None however really had the range of talent or the degree of savvy that Bumps projected.

Bumps had a sense of humor too.

One afternoon he entered the busy Daily Journal offices clutching a heavy briefcase at his side.

"Can we go to the conference room, Reed?", he said sternly, glancing worriedly from side to side. "This is a confidential matter."

"Sure," I snapped, jumping from my chair and grabbing my notebook. Swiftly I led the way to small conference room thinking about all those headline news possibilities that were about to be uncovered.

"Close that door Reed," he ordered.

Once the door closed, Bumps dramatically dumped the entire contents of briefcase on the conference table. Polaroid photographs spilled out everywhere, hundreds of them. All were pornographic."

"We arrested this couple, they were selling photographs of themselves. Right out of the brief case," he said. "Thought you might need some illustrations to go with that story," he added still straight-faced.

I was speechless.

But this time it was the Klan that prompted the visit. Still the Bumps humor was ever present.

"I hear you're getting to be a regular fellow with the Klan, Reed. Have they gotten you your own sheet yet?"

Bumps knew better.

"I think these guys are for real," I told him in all seriousness.

"They are very much for real," he added. He told me, what I already knew, that state police had people very much involved with monitoring the Klan in the Indianapolis area and so far they didn't like what they saw going on inside the Klan.

Bumps hinted at an undercover operation, but carefully avoided any specifics. Well and good. Certainly I didn't want to know anything that could even remotely be in my thoughts as I encountered various Klan figures. Likewise I was not asked too many pressing details of my own Klan encounters Eventually during the conversation Bumps wondered if someone would be allowed to go with me in the future to the 'non-public' sessions of the Klan.

"Chaney has always said I was more than welcome to bring a friend," I answered.

We both agreed to think about it.

Robert M. Reed

A few days later Bumps got back to me on the telephone.

"Still interested in taking a friend to the meetings?," he asked.

"Sure," I agreed, thinking it wouldn't be all that big of a deal to bring someone to the next business meeting of the Klan.

"So does that mean somebody from the outside, like the Indianapolis Police Department?"

Bumps couldn't hold back a chuckle.

"Hell, half of those Indianapolis cops probably already belong to the Klan," he mused.

As it turned out my 'friend' was a rather mild mannered police officer on the Greenwood Police Department. He was new to the force and somehow to me looked much more like a plumber I use to know than a police officer. We met that night shortly after dark at a Greenwood street intersection, after the authorities agreed to my request that the officer not bring a weapon or a badge on the journey. The actual Klan meeting itself was more-or-less routine. I introduced my friend by his proper name but not by actual profession. All the Klan members were polite and hospitable as the meeting ended. Chaney was especially pleasant to me and my mystery guest.

The Grand Dragon himself telephoned me at the newspaper office the next day.

"Glad you could visit us," he cheerily told me of the previous evening's event. "Ya know, you're welcome anytime."

"And," he paused to add, "you're welcome to bring that Greenwood policeman friend of yours anytime too."

I decided right then I didn't have much of a career in the undercover business.

Night of the Klan, A Reporter's Story

Figure 1 *Daily Journal* newspaper account of KKK parade in central Indiana, July 24, 1967.

Robert M. Reed

Knights OF THE Ku Klux Klan

WILL PRESENT A PROGRAM

September 9 & 10
Sumter, S. C.

PLENTY OF ENTERTAINMENT

2 BIG DAYS OF RALLYING AND MUSICAL ENTERTAINMENT — IMPERIAL WIZARD AND MANY GRAND DRAGONS WILL SPEAK — ENTERTAINMENT BEGINS 10:00 A. M. SATURDAY, SEPTEMBER 9 — UNTIL —
MIKE HIGHT AND HIS BAND — PLUS SEVERAL OTHER BANDS AND GROUPS.
AT BUCKEYE PLANTATION — HIGHWAY 521, SOUTH OF SUMTER, S. CAROLINA

Come Hear The Truth
Several Good Speakers

The White Public Is Invited

Authorized By The Board Of Directors The United Klans Of America, Inc.
National Office: Suite 401, Alston Building, Tuscaloosa, Alabama
S. C. Office: Box 4144, Spartanburg, S. C.

Figure 2 Knights of Ku Klux Klan poster for 1960's rally. Authorized by United Klans of America.

Night of the Klan, A Reporter's Story

Figure 3 Parking lot for 1969 Klan rally at isolated location in Indiana. (From smuggled film canister.)

Robert M. Reed

Figure 4 Grand Dragon William Chaney speaks to a group at Indiana Klan rally. (From smuggled film cannister.)

Night of the Klan, A Reporter's Story

Figure 5 Klan leader in full costume at Brown County, Indiana rally in 1969. (From smuggled film canister.)

Robert M. Reed

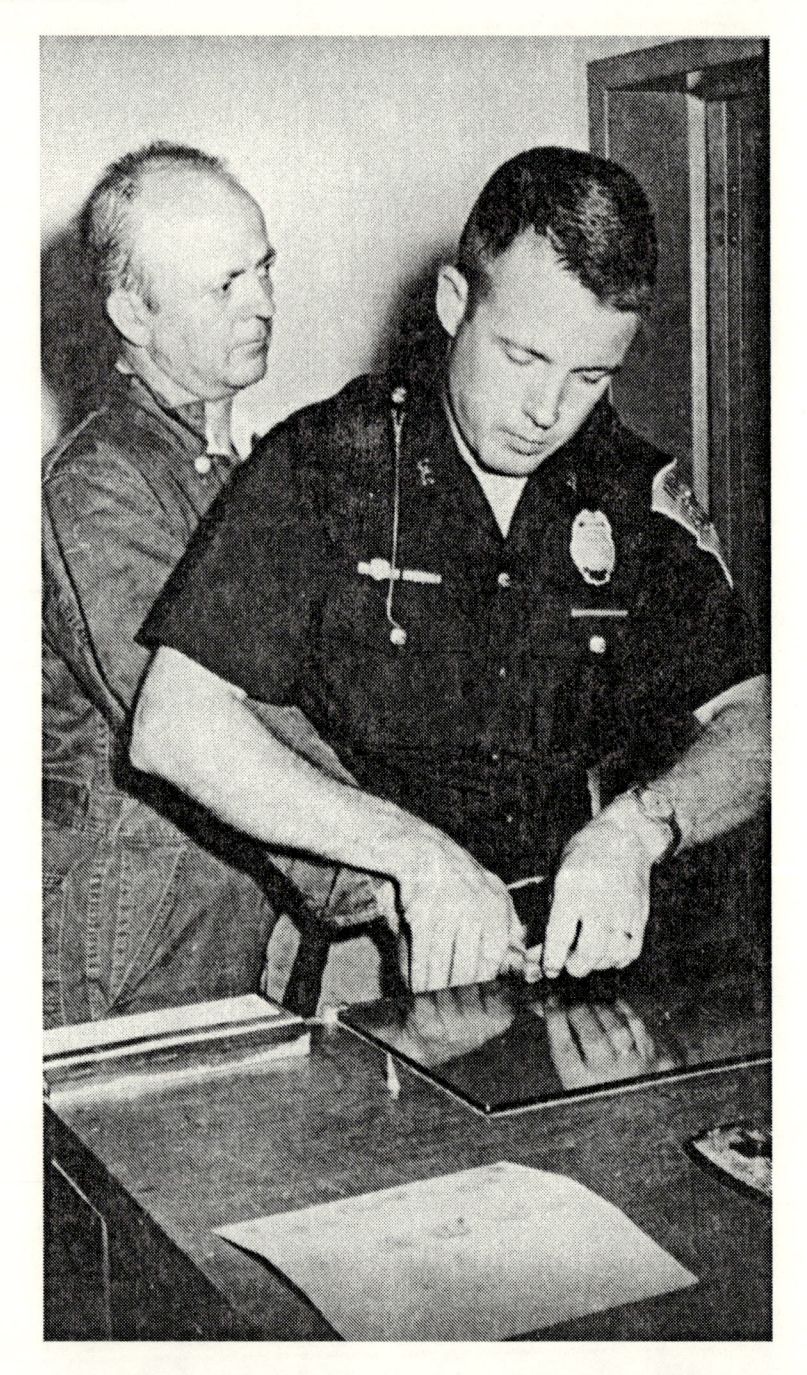

Figure 6 Klan guard booked into jail by Indiana State Police officer following arrest for armed assault at 1969 rally.

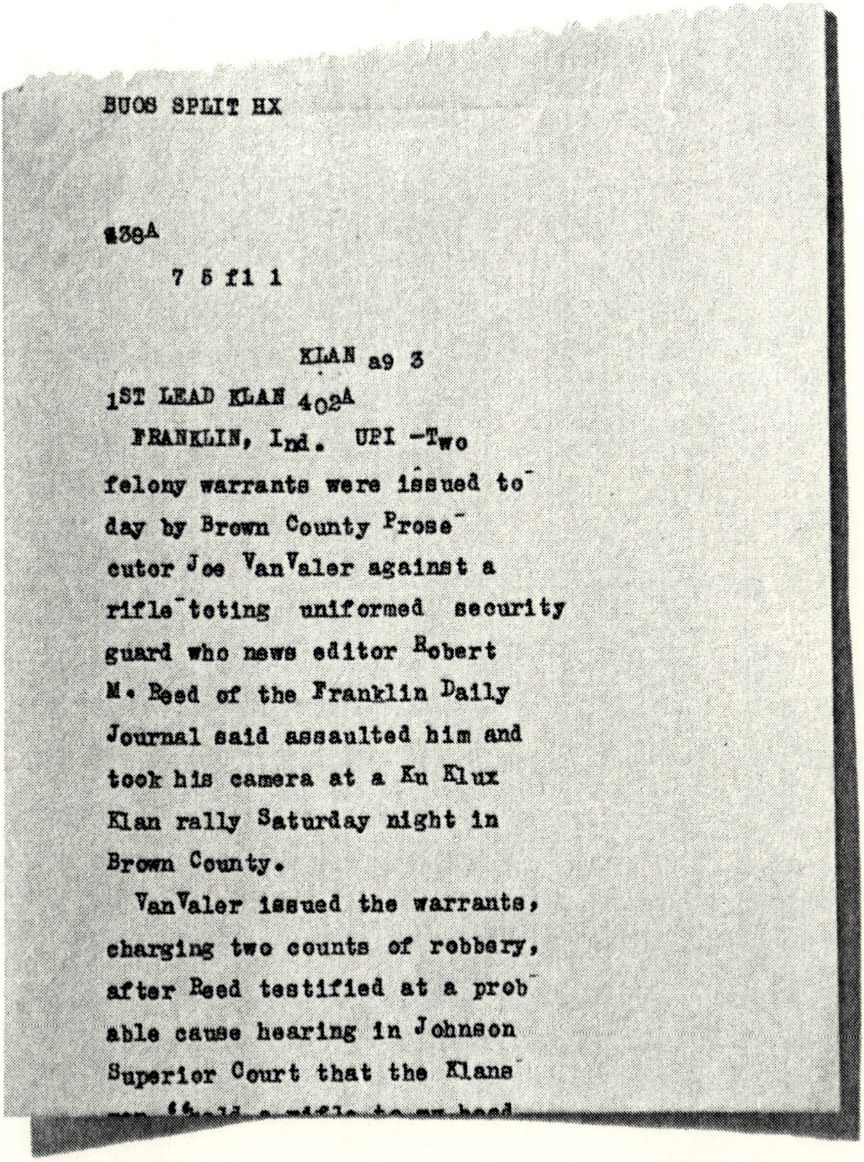

Night of the Klan, A Reporter's Story

```
BUOS SPLIT HX


a39A
    7 5 f1 1


                KLAN a9 3
1ST LEAD KLAN 4o2A
    FRANKLIN, Ind. UPI -Two
felony warrants were issued to-
day by Brown County Prose-
cutor Joe VanValer against a
rifle-toting uniformed security
guard who news editor Robert
M. Reed of the Franklin Daily
Journal said assaulted him and
took his camera at a Ku Klux
Klan rally Saturday night in
Brown County.
    VanValer issued the warrants,
charging two counts of robbery,
after Reed testified at a prob-
able cause hearing in Johnson
Superior Court that the Klans-
```

Figure 7 United Press International teletype message regarding the felony warrants issued for Klan guard charged with assault, September 3, 1969.

Robert M. Reed

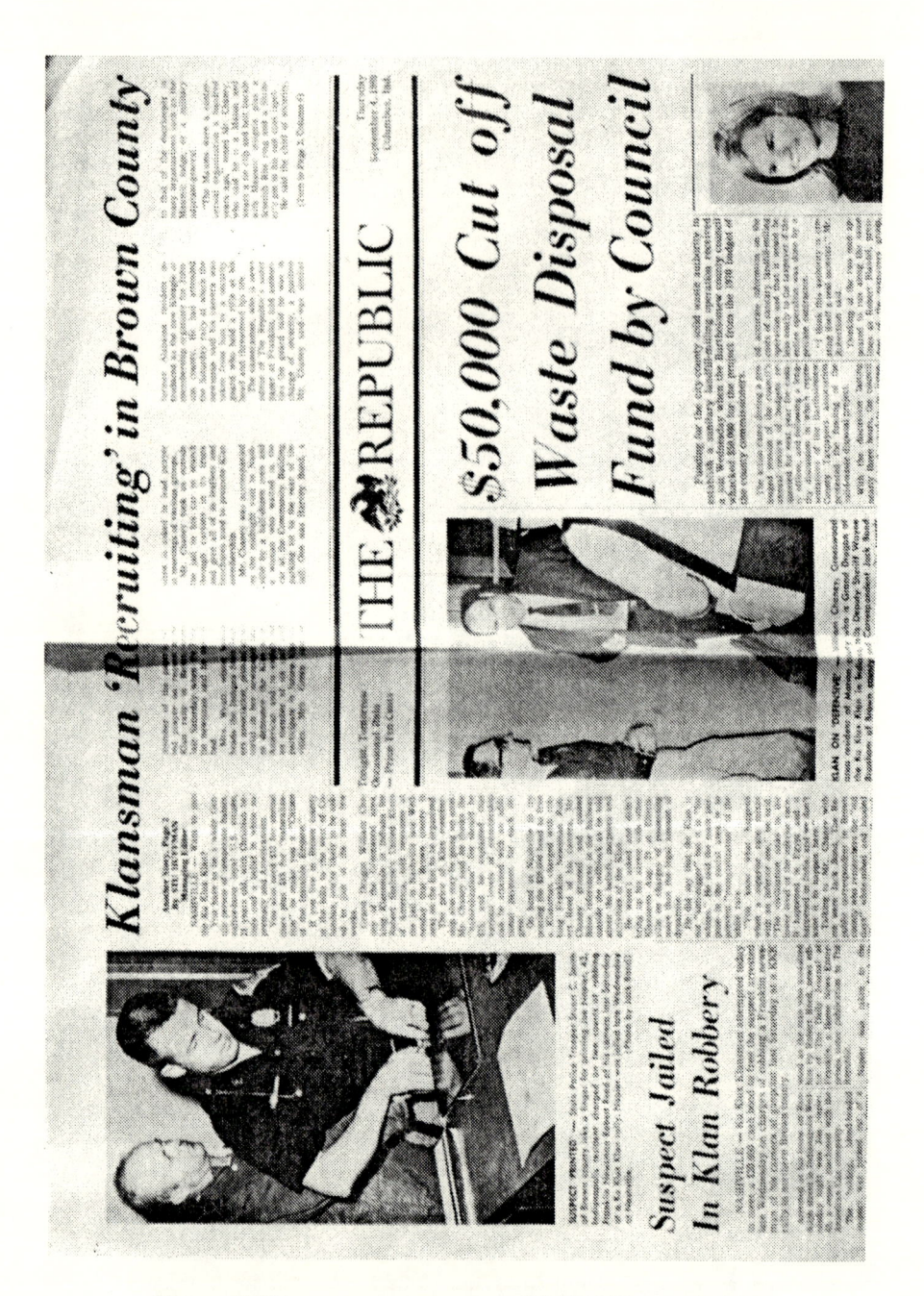

Figure 8 Newspaper coverage of 1969 Klan activities, from *Columbus* (Indiana) *Republic.*

Night of the Klan, A Reporter's Story

Figure 9 Ku Klux Klan truck leads 1967 caravan on U.S. 31 in Franklin, Indiana.

Robert M. Reed

UNITED KLANS OF AMERICA, INC.
"non silba - sed anthar"
REALM OF INDIANA

FROM THE DRAGONS DEN

P. O. BOX 426
GREENWOOD, INDIANA

August 17, 1969

Esteemed Klansmen and Klansladies;

Rally time is approaching again. The Brown County Klanspeople and the Sixth Province, Realm of Indiana, United Klans of America, Inc., Knights of the Ku Klux Klan, will sponser a Rally on 30 Aug., 1969, at 5:30 P. M. , on the Old Zimmermann Farm, on the Spearsville Road, seven miles south of Samaria.

To reach the Old Zimmerman Farm, take Indiana State Route 135 to Samaria, a village mid-way between Trafalger and Morgantown, then take Spearsville Road (first road west of the Samaria Church), seven miles, South.

This Rally will be an "Old Fashion Patriotic Rally", with the theme–Courage is Contagious. We're having a Pitch-in Dinner, Music by the Bob Greens' and others. We have numerous speakers scheduled, who put the love of God, Country, and Race, in its proper perspective.

All White Americans are invited, except those who have left the Order in bad standing, and those who have caused disturbances at previous Rallies. Bring out the family, and invite your relatives and friends.

All Units have your Security guardsmen present in uniform. Instruct them to report to Joe Napier, Chief of Security, on arrival. All other Klanspeople should bring their robes.

Again, I remind you that no alcoholic beverages, nor those under the influence, will be permitted on the Rally grounds. Please so advise our invited guest.

All press releases on the Rally are to be made by the State office.

Your's for God, Country, and Race,

Wm. M. Chaney, Grand Dragon
Phone 1-317-881-4493

P. S. Now! Y'All Come. Sure. W. M. C.
P. S. S. We're having a giant Cross Burning at the conclusion of the program. W. M. C.

Figure 10 Grand Dragon's letter regarding Klan rally in Brown County, Indiana on August 17, 1969.

EVENING

chapter 4

Even by avoiding any further Klan meetings it was apparent that the Klan in Indiana and surrounding areas was increasing it underground activities. Klansmen who stopped by the newspaper office talked less and less of public events and more and more of the force of arms. They had little comment on fellow Klansmen who had already faced criminal charges.

On November 29 of 1967 in Montgomery, Alabama a deputy United States marshal officially advised the regional office of the FBI that two very well known prisoners had surrendered to his office. Eugene Thomas and Collie Leroy Wilkins had appeared there at 8 a.m. on a final stop before going to federal prison. The two former members of the United Klans of America had exhausted their appeals in connection with their convictions in the shooting death of civil rights worker Viola Liuzzo. Under orders of U.S. District judge Frank Johnson, Jr. they were to be transported immediately to the United States Penitentiary in Atlanta, Georgia.

Another party to the shooting of Viola Liuzzo was of course not in the group. Gary Thomas Rowe, a long time Klan member and apparently an equally long time FBI informer as well, was in hiding somewhere in the United States under the protection of Federal authorities. Rowe, as the result of his cooperation with the FBI and his repeated court testimony, never faced criminal charges in connection with the murder case and never would. On the other hand living in fear of vengeance by the Klan, Rowe was also serving a sentence of sorts living with a new name and a secret identity.

As it turned out one of the Federal prisoners Wilkins, was about to be sent into the territory of Indiana Grand Dragon William Chaney. A message dispatched to the FBI office in Mobile, Alabama noted the abrupt change of events:

"Both individuals (Thomas and Wilkins) were transported at the same time to the United States Penitentiary in Atlanta, Georgia. Upon arrival Wilkins was not accepted by prison officials there, and he was returned to Montgomery. He is now scheduled to be delivered to the Federal Correctional Institution, in Terre Haute, Indiana, for confinement."

In Indiana the federal prison in Terre Haute was little more than an hour's westerly drive from Indianapolis. Whether Wilkins, who remained in very good standing with Imperial Wizard Shelton and various other Klan leaders, was actually visited by Klan members is doubtful. Certainly individual Klan leaders or spokesmen seemed to travel about the Midwest with frequency in that period of time and well into the following year.

One spring afternoon in 1968 I received a visit from a Klansman who identified himself as a Kleagle for the United Klans of America from the Cincinnati area. A Kleagle served as a field organizer whose main job was to recruit new members. It was not generally mentioned, but it was understood that the Kleagle received a commission of around three dollars from each new member Klan initiation fee. On this visit the Ohio representative was playing down membership in general and recruiting in particular.

"We don't consider our numbers that important in Ohio," he calmly told me. "We stay concentrated on effects. We think in terms of machine guns and dynamite rather than worry about how big our chapter is."

The Grand Dragon of Georgia Calvin Craig had been quoted in newspapers of the middle 1960s with a hauntingly similar point of view. "I can take five men in a city of 25,000, and that is just like having an army. The five can almost control the political atmosphere of that city."

To me at the time it seemed that the Klan in the Indiana and the Midwest had perhaps taken a much more militant turn, after apparently recruiting enough numbers to carry out various operations.

Besides a part of the membership dues and initiation fees, the Klan realms could also fetch some income by selling robes to new members. Rumor had it that Imperial Wizard Robert Shelton himself received a commission for the nationwide sale of robes and that they were all manufactured at a plant in Columbia, South Carolina. Part of robe revenues also reportedly went to local Klans. The cozy deal apparently ended because Chaney and others within the national leadership strongly suspected that someone within the manufacturing operation was passing along the names and addresses of Klan members who ordered robes for themselves or members of their families to federal authorities. Eventually robe production was 'decentralized' and jobbed out with various state or regional realms.

Revenues from these sources and others, including passing the hat at meetings for assorted defense funds, provided the Klan organization in the latter 1960s with enough resources to enlist lawyers too. Grand Dragon Chaney explained to me that the Indiana Realm of the United Klans of America could draw upon the services of a number of legal representatives if necessary. The most powerful among them was attorney J.B. Stoner. Jesse Benjamin Stoner had long been legal counsel for the national organization of the United Klans of America, and was also legal counsel and executive officer of the National States Rights Party. Even after Chaney left the UKA organization in the 1970s and became Imperial Wizard of the Confederation of Independent Klans he maintained a close association with Stoner.

Night of the Klan, A Reporter's Story

From time to time Chaney would mention brief trips to the South to visit Shelton or Stoner, or sometimes both. At the time the very few details seemed quite insignificant. History of course gave them a new and alarming prospective. It was Stoner who was counsel for the United Klans of America's Michigan Grand Dragon Robert Miles in connection with school bus bombings in Pontiac, Michigan. It was Stoner who represented Byron de la Beckwith who was tried for the murder of Megar Evers. It was Stoner who represented Pennsylvania Grand Dragon Roy Frankhouser when Frankhouser was arrested on charges of trying to sell 240 pounds of explosives to the Michigan Realm of the United Klans of America. And it was Stoner of course who provided assistance and counsel for Thomas Tarrants, the Klansman who was eventually convicted of an attempted bombing of the home of a Jewish church leader in Meridian, Mississippi. Beckwith, Frankhouser and Tarrants among others were all at one time or another fellow members of Stoner's National States Rights Party.

One summer evening in 1968, Meridian police had been posted in a secluded area near the home of Meyer Davidson. They had learned that Davidson and his family might be in danger because of his role in raising reward money in connection with the dynamite bombing of the Beth Israel Congregation Synagogue the previous year. Shortly after midnight they watched a vehicle drive by and then return to a point near the Davidson home. As they watched a man emerged from car carrying heavy box. Police swarmed in to arrest the subject who promptly dropped the box and fled the scene. Inside the box authorities found 29 sticks of dynamite expertly fashioned into a very large explosive device. After a major car chase and a gun battle a seriously wounded Tarrants was arrested. His companion, Kathy Ainsworth a schoolteacher and Klan follower, had been killed by the gunfire.

In November of 1968, Tarrants was convicted of the attempted bombing of a residence and sentenced to the Mississippi State Prison in Parchman, Mississippi. In July of 1969 Tarrants and two companions escaped from that prison and hid out in a rural area near Jackson, Mississippi. Two days later, Federal Bureau of Investigation agents, acting on a tip, confronted the escapees. Their isolated encampment was well fortified with two pistols, two rifles, five hand grenades, and several hundred pounds of ammunition. Despite the firepower, Tarrants and one inmate surrendered with out a fight. The remaining convict foolishly tried to shoot it out and was killed in the gunfire. He was later identified as Louis Shadoan, 46 of Indianapolis, Indiana.

While Stoner had risen to full power in the summer of 1969 now as chairman of the National States Rights Party while remaining chief UKA counsel, another former ally of the United Klans of America was in hiding under the protection of federal authorities. Thomas Rowe, Jr. a Klansman turned FBI informant had testified against his fellow Klansmen in connection with the murder of a civil rights worker in March of 1965 near Selma, Alabama. According to Rowe he had been in an automobile with UKA members William Orville Eaton, Eugene Thomas, and Collie Wilkins when he spotted a car driven by a white woman carrying a black teenager as a passenger. All four men had deep connections with the Klan organization. Rowe had been a member of the Eastview Klavern for a number of years. Eaton, Thomas, and Wilkins were all active members of the Bessemer Klavern and closely associated with Imperial Wizard Shelton. The four Klansmen gave chase to the car as it raced along an isolated stretch of Highway 80 between Selma and Montgomery, Alabama. Their speed was said to have reached 100 miles per hour.

Ultimately Rowe delivered this chilling eyewitness account:

"Gene (Thomas) shouted 'Get 'em' and our car pulled along side of them.

"Extending his arm out of the window, Wilkins rested his elbow on the frame and I thought he intended to shoot out the tires. Gene speeded up still more. Just as Wilkin's arm was almost even with the front window of the woman's automobile, she turned her head and looked at us. I guess the only thing she could see was the muzzle of his gun—the most awful expression came over her face that God knows I've ever seen in my life—and in that instant Wilkins fired two shots at her head.

"I saw the man beside her lean forward, look at us, and then throw his hands over his face, grab the side of his head, and fall over against the dashboard. His body slumped sideways toward the woman's lap, and her body leaned over his. Then all I could see was grass cracking and splintering and all I could hear was gunfire. As we passed the car, Wilkins and Easton emptied their guns at the windshield."

The murder victim was later identified as Viola Liuzzo, a Michigan housewife and mother of five children who had been involved from time to time in civil rights causes. Remarkably, her passenger, 19-year-old civil rights demonstrator Leroy Moton was not seriously injured. He apparently survived by slumping over in the seat and pretending to be dead.

Once Rowe telephoned his secret contacts at the FBI and related the events of earlier that evening, a great cat and mouse game began between federal authorities and the United Klans of America. In some ways it loomed even larger than the tragic death of the Michigan civil rights worker. Rowe and his fellow Klansmen were arrested shortly after his secret call to the FBI, but things did not seem to go according to standard procedure. Rowe was isolated from the group, and when the other three Klansmen were released on bond Rowe was strangely absent. As FBI informants watched

Night of the Klan, A Reporter's Story

Thomas, Easton, and Wilkins immediately huddled with attorney Matt Murphy and Imperial Wizard Shelton. One of the major items of discussion was why Rowe was not being arraigned in court at the same time as the others. Later Rowe explained his absence from the group meeting with Murphy and Shelton by telling others he was just driving around.

The degree of the Klan's concern was revealed in a highly confidential memorandum sent from FBI operatives in Alabama superiors in Washington. In late March of 1965 it noted, "the subjects and other Klan associates have been making an obvious effort to determine if there was an informant in this matter, and if so, to identify him... Investigation of the conspiracy is being aggressively pursued."

While a furious Klan searched for an informer within their ranks, the FBI had whisked Rowe away to a hiding place in California. Shelton had a very strong inkling that Rowe was the 'rat fink' from within but his followers could not fully confirm it. Finally, by early April, leaks in the news media began to openly suggest that the FBI had made arrests in the murder of the civil rights worker so quickly because of 'inside' help. On April 7, 1965 a national radio commentator suggested, undoubtedly based on comments from FBI sources, that the FBI had indeed a highly placed informant and that the informant was actually in the Klan automobile at the time of the shooting. While FBI memorandums at the time noted the broadcast in detail, the agency made no effort to deny the report. (Of course the FBI also never dealt with the obvious moral issue of whether the FBI informant should have acted to prevent the fatal shooting of an innocent victim. The same basic moral issue was also apparently ignored by the FBI a few years later when I was the victim of armed Klansmen.)

By late April of 1965 the story was out everywhere that Rowe was the long-suspected informer that that he would be a key witness in the prosecution of his former fellow Klansman. As public furor developed over the use of an "undercover agent" in such an operation, the United States Justice Department made efforts to inform the news media that while trained FBI agents were sometimes used to infiltrate groups such as the Klan, non-agent informers were also used. In the Civil Rights murder case, they contended, the informer was a Klansman who had regularly supplied information to the FBI for sometime. Both FBI Director Hoover and Attorney General Katzenbach boasted, both on and off the record, that use of such insider Klan informants was quite successful.

"At times," Attorney General Katzenbach told reporters at one point in the 1960s, "I think we know more about what the Klan is doing than we know about what some divisions of the Justice Department are doing."

What the United Klans of America was doing in the weeks immediately after the arrest of Thomas, Easton, and Wilkins was contacting various

Klaverns to solicit support, moral and financial, for the accused Klansmen. One or more of the trio appeared before various Klan groups evoking cheers and applause. Contributions to their defense flowed in from various sources. A restaurant owner in Ft. Pierce, Florida reportedly collected $600 in free will donations to be used for defense attorneys. A informant for the FBI was quoted in reports as saying that based on his past knowledge he doubted if all or even any of the money actually reached UKA headquarters in Alabama. No matter what amount eventually reached the Imperial Wizard, the defense attorneys were able to do quite well in the climate that then prevailed in Alabama.

Wilkins, for example, was eventually tried on state charges of murder in Lowndes County courthouse. Imperial Wizard Shelton assisted defense attorney Matt Murphy throughout the trial. When the jury became deadlocked the court declared a mistrial and Wilkins was freed on bond. As the night ended Wilkins climbed into Shelton's black Cadillac and disappeared. The following day Shelton, Eaton and Wilkins appeared in a Klan parade in Anniston, Alabama. As the parade cars moved along Wilkins waved a confederate flag and the crowd of several hundred clapped their hands and hooted in approval.

Once Rowe telephoned his contacts the FBI, the four Klansmen were immediately arrested. Federal authorities granted Rowe immunity for his testimony and Eaton died of natural causes before authorities could obtain a conviction. After being finally acquitted in state court on murder charges individually, Wilkins and Thomas were eventually convicted on lesser federal civil rights violations and sentenced to ten years in prison. At the time federal authorities lamented that full-measure law enforcement against the Klan was very unlikely.

"Crimes are committed that are never reported in the press, never investigated by the local law," said one federal agent. "The victims, if they survived, are afraid to file a complaint. In the event an arrest is made and a man is brought to trial, getting a conviction is almost impossible."

Rowe had long since disappeared under what would eventually become the federal witness protection program and remained 'invisible' to the Invisible Empire and most everyone else. The FBI managed to kept Rowe out of sight and at the very same time keep a close watch on Klan reactions. Such reactions were not long in coming. In late April this urgent teletype message was sent from FBI headquarters in Washington to a number of regional offices:

"On April 25 last, (censored) advised that in (censored) South Carolina, Grand Dragon Bob Scoggins exhibited the photograph of Rowe, the FBI informant in Selma, Alabama, and instructed all Grand Officers, Exalted Cyclops and Titans of the Klan to be on the lookout for him. If this individual is located the Grand Dragon is to be immediately notified of his whereabouts.

"Informant advised that this meant that 'the gun is out for him' as an 'FBI fink' and that he will be taken care of for lying. He (informant) also advised that the Klan is trying to locate the family of Rowe, however, he did not know why they wanted his family but probably wanted to harass them to find out where Rowe is located."

Once-confidential records show the FBI at the time took the information vary seriously and rapidly notified their regional offices of the potential for violence. As seriously as they took the information that made no effort to muzzle any of the Klan including Scoggins himself. As a matter of fact Scoggins made frequent trips to Indiana and other parts of the Midwest. Scoggins attended a number of Grand Dragon Chaney's Midwest organizational meetings in the years immediately following. The Klan technique of singling out targets at secret sessions and threatening group retaliation came to be a standard operation for the Klan groups. As I would eventually personally learn the Klan leadership was especially interested in seeking out possible family members of whomever seemed to be a threat to them at the time. Years later Rowe would also document much of the same Klan operation in a book on the subject. Unfortunately ex-Klansman Rowe was not available for comment that particular spring and summer.

Sources within the Klan and elsewhere in the 1960s indicated that rather than involve the Klan organization directly, the group would use what were known was 'wrecking crews' to take on risky ventures that could well fall outside of the law. Typically the wrecking crews were selected from various klaverns to comprise a group of three or four members for such secret missions. Often the crew members, being from separate klaverns, did not previously know each other. Further, Klan ranking officers were rarely, if ever a part of the crew mission.

In late July of 1969, Grand Dragon Chaney made a bit of news himself when he was arrested while on Klan business in Michigan on the charge of carrying a concealed weapon.

"I intended to defend my family and my convictions with all the resources at my command," he defiantly commented after his release on bond. Rather than family members however the car that Chaney was riding in at the time of his arrest contained three members of the Michigan Knights of the Ku Klux Klan.

During that same summer period Chaney had not made his usual visits to the newspaper office in Franklin. No small wonder. He was obviously busy with his Klan duties elsewhere. Shortly after midnight on Thursday, August 12 law enforcement officers from the Monroe County Sheriff's office drove to a residence near Ellettsville, Indiana a small town north of

Bloomington. They were in hopes of serving a burglary warrant on 27-year-old Jack Kinser. At the time Kinser was being sought in connection with a hardware store burglary in neighboring Brown County where firearms and ammunition were among the items taken. Moreover Kinser was out on bond after being arrested for the firebombing of a market in Bloomington. And further, in November of the previous year he had been arrested in connection with burglary of a Bedford hardware store in which $7,000 worth of firearms was stolen. Given the suspect's background, the sheriff's officers were understandably wary. Had they known what else was waiting for them at that location they would have been even more wary.

As the four officers descended on the location they found not only Kinser behind the house near a shed but four other men with him. In front of them was an opened box containing 14 sticks of dynamite. Turning flashlights inside the shed they found six unopened 50 pound boxes of dynamite. Inside they also found an electric detonator, a bushel basket of dynamite caps, and a welding torch. All together they carefully confiscated 328 pounds of dynamite. Their suspects were impressive too. Indiana Grand Dragon Chaney, Kleagle of Province 7 Johnny Stancombe of Bloomington, King Kleagle Paul Book of Kokomo, Indiana, and Klan Klaiff Jimmie Elvis Bass also of Kokomo, and the man they had been originally searching all along for Jack Kinser.

All five were taken to jail in Bloomington. By Thursday evening Chaney had been able to post $5,000 bond. The others remained in the Monroe County jail. As an afterthought, Circuit Court judge Nat U. Hill raised Kinser's bond to $20,000. Chaney and the others swore later that the sheriff's officers had been tipped off in advance. The police officers, meanwhile steadfastly insisted they knew nothing of the dynamite or the Klansmen when they went to the residence in search of the burglary suspect.

In the days that followed the Monroe County prosecutor said the explosives had been taken from a number of construction sites in Bloomington and as far away as Columbus, Indiana. "Dynamite leaves no evidence," Alabama attorney general Richmond Flowers had declared earlier during his own investigation of the United Klans of America, "it has a paralyzing psychological effect, and the wrecking crew can be 20 miles away then the blast goes off." Obviously the Klan had no intentions of clearing away that many tree stumps anytime in the near future.

Less than a week after the incident I received a letter from the United Klans of America, Realm of Indiana. Sometime long before I had been placed on their membership mailing list. The letter read:

"Esteemed Klansmen and Klansladies:

"Rally time is approaching again. The Brown County Klanspeople and the Sixth Province, Realm of Indiana, United Klans of America, Inc.,

Night of the Klan, A Reporter's Story

Knights of the Klu Klux Klan will sponsor a Rally on 30 Aug., 1969 at 5:30 p.m., on the Old Zimmerman Farm, on the Spearsville, a village mid-way between Trafalgar and Morgantown, then take Spearsville Road, seven miles, South.

"This Rally will be and Old Fashion Patriotic Rally, with the theme— Courage Is Contagious. We're having a Pitch-in Dinner, Music by Bob Greens' and others. We have numerous speakers scheduled, who put the love of God, Country, and Race, in its proper perspective.

"All White Americans are invited, except those who have left the Order in bad standing, and those who have caused disturbances at previous Rallies. Bring out the family, and invite your relatives and friends.

"All Units have your Security guardsmen present in uniform. Instruct them to report to Joe Napier, Chief of Security, on arrival. All other Klanspeople should bring their robes.

"Again, I remind you that no alcoholic beverages, nor those under the influence will be permitted on the Rally grounds. Please so advise our invited guests.

"All press releases on the Rally are to be made by the State office."

It was signed "yours for God, Country, and Race" William Chaney, Grand Dragon. Beneath the signature was his telephone number.

When I called, he immediately answered.

"That thing in Bloomington was simply a misunderstanding, ya know," he said in response to my questions. "I am told, that these things sometimes happen," Chaney added calmly as though he had simply been mistaken for someone else at a family reunion picnic.

Wondering if I was any longer welcome at Klan activities, I asked if it would be alright if I attended the rally.

Oh yeah, sure," Chaney quickly boomed. "Bring your wife, you'll be welcome."

I didn't recall mentioning to the Grand Dragon or his fellow Klansmen that I even had wife. But I could have. And it could easily have come up in his conversation with most anyone else who knew me.

"And don't for get to bring your camera," Chaney added to my parting comments.

Seems like I'd heard that request before.

I immediately telephoned Claudette to tell we would need a baby sitter on Saturday evening, because I was taking her out to dinner. She was pleased. I decided to leave out the Klan rally part of it until later.

Robert M. Reed

NIGHTFALL

chapter 5

What would become a memorable evening for my wife and me began with a quite dinner in at a place called Lum's. In late August of 1969 the restaurant chain had just opened a location in near by Greenwood, and it was moderately priced.

Claudette was still not completely sold on the idea of going to a Klan rally in the Brown County wilderness as our 'date' for the evening. I used the 'fun' word often as we dined that evening. The rally would give Claudette a chance to see these Klan folks that I had long talked about in person and probably in full Klan costume. Besides, I added, the event was right out there in the open unlike all the closed meetings that I had attended. And Chaney had made a point of not only inviting me but suggesting my spouse would be welcome too. These Klansmen were questionable characters, I admitted, but Chaney has always kept them under control. Nothing dangerous tonight was planned tonight, just a sort of family picnic with the added attraction of a cross burning.

"And what fool," I questioned, "would take his beloved wife along on anything with even the slightest risk?"

Claudette looked directly in my eyes and smiled, making her point very well without ever saying it out loud.

We took a leisurely drive southward on US 31. At Amity, about five miles south of Franklin we turned on State Road 252 and headed westward toward Samaria. At Trafalgar the highway merged with State Road 135 and we continued the next few sparsely populated miles until we came upon Samaria. Samaria was only a tiny grouping of a few houses and a meager auto repair garage. The only landmark, the Samaria Church, was a familiar one to me. My grandfather used to be the minister at the small, community church and I had spent many a Sunday afternoon playing in the church-yard while various social events were hosted within the church. I was much less familiar with the landscape as we at last turned off of the highway and onto the Spearsville Road. By any standards it was a back road used only by the few who then lived in the area, and it became more and more remote as we drove. It was fortunate that the Klan had posted small directional posters along the route. Most of them were simply nailed to trees.

Our route continued about seven miles on the blacktop road before coming to still another Klan poster directing us onto a small gravel road. We drove slowly through a heavily wooded area with not a house in sight, and I

Night of the Klan, A Reporter's Story

told Claudette I was glad the evening sun was still shining as we searched for the site of the rally. The narrowing road led through what seemed to be a dry creek bed, over a hill and right up to a two story farm house. The mailbox at the road had a small American flag on top of it, and a small Confederate flag along the side of it.

The Old Zimmerman farm, as it turned out, belonged to someone who was not named Zimmerman at all but the farm had retained the name in that part of the country although the former owner who had long since died. Cars were parked in a small field next to the house. It was shortly before 7 p.m. and already there were about three of four rows of cars in the area. One pickup truck in the front row bore a plate on the front that read, "Support Your Local Klan." I knew we had the right place. There was no greeting committee. We just parked the car and made our way among the parked cars. People were moving about in the improvised parking lot. Some of the cars had their trunks open and the two of us were immediately struck by sight of so many firearms in one location.

"God," Claudette whispered as she nudged my, "they've got guns everywhere."

And they did. Immediately in front of us were two uniformed Klan security guards, one of which I recognized from the earlier Klan meetings in Indianapolis. Both of them wore Klan patches on their gray shirts, Klan emblems on their white helmet liners, and unmarked combat boots. They hardly noticed us. Both were busy loading rifles from boxes of ammunition in the trunk of one vehicle. In a sworn deposition sometime later, a Klan follower who was at the rally that evening would testify to a conversation in that field with someone he thought to be an undercover police officer. He said the 'undercover' agent had remarked too about so many guns floating around there.

"He had seen my pistol and he had seen another one I had unwrapped to show to another guy I was thinkin' about trading with. So I took the hint and wrapped it back up and put it in the trunk and locked it up."

Upon further questioning, he recalled seeing lots of weapons at the Brown County rally despite Grand Dragon Chaney's earlier orders to the contrary.

"I remember hearing Mr. Chaney at one time say that he did not want any weapons to be shown at the rallies. But now the people that had pistols that I seen could of very easily been police officers. But most of the ones that I seen was like we'd be off trading guns. If you got an interest in guns and collecting 'em or something, you know a guy that's got access to 'em will always talk to you about guns."

"Everybody carries a gun anymore," he added during his later testimony. "I mean the majority of the free public does. At least what I call the free public carries guns. Personally I think its justified."

That particular testimony would come from what I called one of the 'shadow' Klan. They were clearly Klan supporters and allies, but for whatever reasons did not become full members. They attended the rallies and other public events, but were not invited to the private Klan meetings. Any legal testimony was typically only given very reluctantly and then only after being served with a proper court subpoena. Of the 100 or so people at that August rally, many of them were 'shadow' Klan and very lastingly dedicated to the goals of the KKK.

At the rally site Bob Green's small musical band provided entertainment as followers moved about the grounds. Perhaps 20 to 30 Klansmen were outfitted in various robes. Often the robes were just fitted like doctor's white jacket over their street cloths. A few others however had more elaborate costumes complete with matching hoods. The newly appointed Klan Kagle, later introduced as Harvey Bond, appeared in full regalia including hood. The most elaborated dressed was Grand Dragon Chaney in his flowing green robe, across the chest of the garment was the single word, Indiana.

Presently a gathering of about two-dozen people filled an assortment of folding chairs and kitchen chairs before a makeshift wooden platform. On platform itself was a three-foot cross that was illuminated by Christmas tree bulbs, a KKK flag, and a Confederate flag. At the far edge of the platform stood an American flag. Chaney climbed onto the platform and addressed his rather sparse audience. Dozens of others milled about the grounds as the program began. A few Klan members sat by a card table set up near the platform to enroll new members and sell a few items of Klan memorabilia including bumper stickers and pin-back buttons with the white-lettered word "Never" on a blue background. Helmeted security guards also moved about the grounds. Two or three were wearing gray shirts like the two we had noticed loading rifles, and three or four others wore similar uniforms but with blue shirts. Much later I would learn that the gray shirted guards were from Indiana Klans and the blue shirted guards were from Michigan Klans.

From the platform Chaney was telling the audience, "you don't see too many people here, but this is the first time you've seen a Klan rally in Brown County in more than 30 years. This thing is gonna roll!"

"Brown County used to be on of the strongest Klan areas in the state," he continued. "And I'm sure it will be again. Rallies like this will become more and more of an everyday occurrence. The Klan is back!"

There were hardy cheers and applause from the immediate crowd and from others who were hearing the loudspeakers blare else where on the grounds. Then, in what may have been a veiled threat to prosecutor

Night of the Klan, A Reporter's Story

VanValer, the Grand Dragon declared, "We're going to see this thing through to the end. Politicians that get in our way will be remembered when we come to power."

There was more cheering and applause.

Claudette was sort of left on her own as I walked about the grounds taking notes and also taking pictures of the activities and participants. From time to time a few of the Security Guards were snapping orders at another photographer in attempts to prevent him from taking pictures at some locations. I was given no such warning, but there was a clear sense that some of the Klansmen and most of the Security Guards were becoming uncomfortable with the presence of cameras. In subpoenaed testimony later, one 'shadow' Klan supporter who had attended the rally remembered expressing his concern to the chief of the Security Guards.

"I had mentioned to Mr. Napier that at one time this young joker was running around with an infra ray camera or what you want to call it, taking pictures. One without a flash type."

Years later Klan bodyguard and FBI informant Thomas Rowe, Jr., would document in his book of a fellow KKK guard ripping film out of cameras at a rally. "We gots us a couple of photographers," the guard had breathlessly told Rowe. "They were taking pictures with infra-red light of you and Bobby (Shelton) with the Chief. We though y'all would want the film." Rowe had noted similar incidents in his career as a Klansman, finally concluding, "the only thing a Klansman hates as much as integration is a camera."

But again, in the summer of 1969 ex-guard and ex-informant Rowe was in hiding and not making public comments on anything. Back at the Brown County rally, Chaney had picked up the microphone again, this time to apparently avoid further conflict with the guards and photographers such as myself. "You news reporters are our guests and you make take pictures or anything you wish…just like you're in your own backyard."

"Don't worry about being recognized," he then admonished his follow Klan members. "You'll just fade into the background."

The continued glare of the Security Guards however, was not very assuring at all to me. Warily I slowly made my back to Claudette and slipped a canister of exposed film into her soft hand. "Please hide this," I whispered.

She nodded as if spy missions were daily things for us, and slipped the film canister I had given her into her purse. Claudette anxiously told me in the next moment of a confrontation between two Klan guards and some other photographer. "They were really mad," she insisted, "you'd better watch it 'till we get out of here."

I decided to take her advice.

After the sun had gone down the robed Klansman formed a group and began slowly walking across the road and toward a small hill. Klan followers fell into place behind robed chieftains, and Claudette and I just wandered in the same direction but well behind the rest. By the time we reached the hill, despite the darkness, we could see the crowd gather about handcrafted 20 foot cross. Klansmen in earlier 'talks' had boasted of the construction of these crosses. The wooden frame was wrapped in burlap and bailing wire, then it was saturated in gasoline to ignite it and motor oil to keep it burning. One Klan formula called for two quarts of gasoline for very five quarts of motor oil. Sometimes, it was told, wrecker trucks had to be used to wench the mighty crosses into place. I had no idea how this particular cross was actually erected, but it appeared to be a fairly solid structure.

After a brief ceremony, Chaney and the other robed Klansmen lit torches with rags soaked in apparently the same mixture that would fire the cross. They paraded around for a few more minutes and then ignited the cross. The flames rapidly stretched around the structure giving it a blazing light across the blackened night sky. No wonder the Klan called it the fiery cross, I thought to myself, it truly was.

As the cross burned, the Klansman moved in a circle around the cross. A couple of people began taking pictures. No one objected. I began taking a few pictures too, but the flash attachment on my camera was not working correctly. I was doubtful the resulting artwork would be very worthwhile. As the Klan crowd chanted the song "The Old Rugged Cross," and began experiencing what they termed the 'ring of fire', Claudette and I quietly retreated our steps back down the hill. With the crowd still involved with the cross burning ceremony back on the hill, the field where the cars were parked was nearly deserted. Deserted that is, except for a cluster of Security Guard. This time they were openly carrying rifles as they stood along the edge of the road. As our car eased back through the parking lot I hesitated at the road's edge. Putting the car's transmission into the park position, I left the engine running as I rolled down the car window for a final photograph of the armed Klan guard.

"Alright, that's it. Stop right there," shouted another Security Guard who was already too close to the left side of our car for me to avoid.

I sat there for an instant with the engine running knowing we couldn't possibly outrun the rifle and hoping perhaps that Grand Dragon Chaney's assurance would be enough. I was right about my first guess. And I was very wrong on the second guess.

"Goddam you," he shouted, "I told you not to take any pictures." The barrel of his rifle pushed up against my head.

Much later in time the prosecutor's office evoked this under oath testimony from a Klan supporter who had, for some reason, followed the two of us down the hill that dark night.

"I knew if that Guard pulled the trigger then, why it would have blown that reporter's head off. I know just standing there I was scared shitless."

"And I had no idea if the gun was loaded. I wasn't going to check that far into it. I figured it wasn't none of my business so that was it. 'Cause at the time, I, you know, I was not a member of the Klan, so as far as that goes, I didn't know, you know. This was the first violence that I had seen connected with anything of the Klan, see and I says to myself, Goddamn what the hell is goin' on here?"

•

MIDNIGHT

chapter 6

> Death's Brigade
> Thrice hath the lone owl hooted
> And thrice the panther cried,
> And swifter through the darkness
> The Pale Brigade shall ride.
> No trumpet sounds it coming,
> And no drum-beat stirs the air,
> But noiseless in their vengeance
> They wreak it everywhere.
> Klu Klux.
> -Memphis Avalanche, 1869.

There is something which physiological experts call the life review process. It is the term given to the mental activity some people experience when they believe their death is imminent. In the popular media it is better known as the life-passing-before-your-eyes experience. Those who have been to brink of the abyss are often keenly aware of it. Those who have managed to live their lives without great danger may not fully comprehend this strange process.

With me at the Klan rally at gunpoint it was less of a review and more of a realization.

Whatever type of rifle was lodged up against the side of my head, I judged, would be of sufficient caliber and range to kill Claudette and I both. A trigger pulled in anger or pulled by accident would be just as accurate and just deadly. We would die instantly and just as instantly two little children would be in this world without their parents. The Klan security guard was screeching louder now. Another gray-shirted guard was by his side, he was also armed with a high-caliber rifle. Then a blue-shirted guard appeared. Then another. And another. They immediately surrounded the car and turned their flashlights inside the car lighting the clear fear in our faces.

"I outta blow your godamned head off," the initial Klan guard screamed, using the rifle to shove my head back at sharp angle toward Claudette.

"Chaney said I could take pictures," I stammered with my voice choking.

Night of the Klan, A Reporter's Story

"God Damn you, I told you not to take my picture," he shouted again banging the rifle's barrel against my skin. "I don't care what Chaney said, I'm Chief of Security around here."

"Now gimme that film," he demanded. The guard next to him immediately said, "get the damned camera too."

"Bob, give them the camera," Claudette said softy but firmly, tears flooding her cheeks. I slid my hand across the seat to touch her fingers.

Much later another Klan 'shadow' would give his own testimony under oath which described his view of what happened next that night.

"I was real close by that time, and I could hear the lady who was sittin' in the car say to give them the film. The guard kept poking him with the gun. And I do know that I did actually feel sorry for the newspaper boy. He had three or four security guards right standing right square up against the front of the car.

"Then I heard the round slide in the chamber or something. And it sounded like it was loaded and ready to fire."

Another Klan follower who was also watching that night in the shadows, later also gave sworn statement to authorities after nearly two years of legal proceedings.

"That guard kept the gun right on his head, a' pushing and a' pushing. That reporter he was so damned scared he was just shaking all over. The woman was crying...I think that just a little bit more, if she had been there, sittin there another minute longer, I think she would have been hysterical. Cause she was just right on the verge of it. I know she was cryin' and scared to death."

With his rifle still at my head, the Klan guard snatched the camera from my hands as I attempted to lift it from my lap.

"Now get outta here," he yelled, "If I ever see you at a Klan meeting again I kill you."

The two of us sped off onto the dark gravel road still terrified.

A couple of cars bearing Klansmen pulled off the parking site and fell in behind us. At this point we had no idea what was coming next. We had driven about a quarter-mile when—like a story book ending—we saw a clearly marked Indiana State Police car in a small clearing right on the edge of the road.

I slammed on the brakes and the two Klan cars behind us had to swerve to avoid contact with the rear of my car. The hell with them I thought, the State Police were here, its over.

But it wasn't over. There was no storybook ending.

There was a trooper in the car. He listened at the window as I tried to get myself under control enough to tell him what has just happened.

"What do you expect me to do about?," he said.

I felt like I had just been slapped.

"What, they held us at gun point! The Klan with rifles...I...I," I was stammering.

He waved off my request to at least file a written complaint, saying it wouldn't do any good.

"Don't you even want me to leave my name?"

"No," he said, "it won't be necessary."

Abruptly he suggested he might be able to recover the camera. He spoke briefly into his police radio. Then he drove off in the police car leaving us standing alone in the darkness. More cars from the Klan rally were moving slowly by.

Panic overwhelmed us.

We fled once again on the dark, narrow gravel road.

About a mile down the road the fear eased somewhat and I slowed down. Perhaps we would be safer I reasoned if we went back to find the state police officer. Maybe, I hoped, he was already realizing the full seriousness of this thing and would get us safely home. I turned the car around in the road and headed back toward where we first met the trooper. Darkness and dust choked the road. By the time I arrived back where his patrol car had been, the trooper was waiting there for us. The trooper had my camera but nothing else, again he declined to take any report of the crime. No report on an armed robbery? Not even theft of a camera?

"Look," he said finally and flatly, "you got your camera back didn't you?"

Bitterly disillusioned, we fled the area of the Klu Klux Klan rally for the final time. At least I got the trooper's identification. His nameplate on his uniform said Ackerman.

"I wonder if he came to the rally wearing the wearing the wrong uniform?," I asked Claudette darkly.

"My God," she responded, "is everybody in the Klan?"

Sometime later, again giving testimony under oath, a Klan sympathizer would tell of the trooper returning to the rally site.

The trooper "shined his light and said he wanted the camera, who ever had it. So the guard took it out of his trunk and took the camera over to the police officer. They had a discussion over there, but I couldn't hear it.

"Then the guard came back to the trunk of his car, which was still open, and began taking shells out of a gun in there. He also had two or three other rifles or guns in the back end and told them (fellow Klansmen) to take them home because he was afraid that he might get stopped and have 'em in his car."

As we sped along that dark night we are afraid of being stopped too, by the Klan. I decided we wouldn't stop for anything, or anyone this time until we reached Franklin. I hardly remember most of the rest of the trip, but I do recall Claudette frantically urging me at one point on highway 252 to slowdown. I glanced at the speedometer and realized we have been traveling through the dark night at over 80 miles an hour. Our car swept into the Franklin police station with tires screeching. On duty at the station was Sgt. Clemmet Shepherd, someone I had known since high school. In breathless fashion I once again related the events of the past two hours, including the strange apathy of state trooper Ackerman. Shepherd, a seasoned police officer himself, was astonished. At least he knew a crime when he saw one. Shepherd didn't waste any words in telling me to drive home and immediately contact the prosecutor's office. He suggested calling the Federal Bureau of Investigation as well.

"Be damned careful here," he said, "until you know who's connected with the Klan and who isn't."

If there was any good news, it was that Shepherd was already working the FPD night shift and would be on duty in Franklin the rest of the night. He promised to keep a close watch on our house. I knew he would do that. He was a good cop. At home Claudette rushed a bewildered teenage baby sitter out of the house and toward the car where I was waiting with the motor running. Fortunately the sitter lived only about eight blocks away, but it was a wild ride. With Claudette and the children waiting alone, I was frantic to get back to them. I didn't wait for the poor baby sitter to reach her own front door. I wheeled away with the tires screaming as she stood on the edge of the street.

Back at home I burst through into the front door, panting and worried. Claudette had checked and double-checked on Matthew and Judy. They were both sleeping soundly, blissfully unaware of the danger to their parents. Thank God.

The adrenaline was still raging though my body. We barricaded the front door, using what furniture the two of us could move together. Next I drug out my old softball bat out of the closet and propped it against the wall. I had never owned a firearm and never trusted having them around. In all my childhood my father had never owned a firearm. He admitted that as a farm boy he had sometimes hunted with a squirrel gun, but as far as the household was concerned he felt we were safer without them.

Next I dashed to the telephone and began dialing.

Looking back, I can remember hearing the voice of second thoughts. This little voice in the back of my mind was saying keep your mouth shut and don't risk the wrath and revenge of the Klu Klux Klan. Move on to other quieter things, the voice said. Forget about it.

Alabama Attorney Richmond Flowers had put it this way in writing for a national magazine during the middle 1960s:

"It is no wonder that the average citizen is reluctant to speak up. He knows that if he crossed the Klan, his family may be in danger. His home may be bombed by a self-appointed, social misfit. Since there would be little chance of a conviction, he keeps silent."

For me I was ignoring the voice of second thoughts as well as the voice of attorney general Flowers. Claudette and I were as one on this. The Klan had gone too far. Since I obviously did not have prosecutor Joe VanValer's home telephone, I called the Greenwood Police Department and told them I had an emergency. The dispatcher said prosecutor VanValer was gone for the Labor Day weekend and deputy prosecutor Terry Eads, she thought, was at a party somewhere.

"Listen," I shouted, much louder that I should have, "My wife and I have been held at gun point by the Klu Klux Klan. We got away, but we may still be in trouble. I desperately need to talk to somebody. Now!"

I left my telephone number and deputy prosecutor Eads called me on the phone about ten minutes later. Hurriedly but being as exact as I could, I gave him the details of this night of the Klan. He absorbed the details just as rapidly as I gave them.

"Where are you now?" Eads asked.

I told him we were barricaded in the house.

"Stay there," he said.

Eads said he would make some calls and see what sort of security was available in the county during the night. I suggested we really needed the FBI in on this too. He agreed to check on it. Immediately after the conversation I was on the phone to the Indianapolis office of the FBI. I told my story again to the person the operator transferred my call to, and again left my telephone number. My telephone rang again about 20 minutes later. The caller identified himself as a FBI agent. I told the story still again.

"Have you seen anyone outside your house?", the agent asked.

I dropped the phone. Ran to peer out of the living room windows and ran back again.

"Nothing," I said, breathing heavily, "nothing so far."

The FBI agent gave me a special telephone number and urged me not to panic.

"We'll have some people available," the agent noted. "If there is a problem just make the call and we can be there in no time." He made no mention of calling local police, or even state police, if there was trouble. Hell, I thought to myself, it there's trouble I'm calling everybody. Everybody, including the United States Army too, if I could reach them on the phone. Thumbing through the telephone book I swore that if the Klan got to us that night they'd have to pry the telephone from my one hand while my other hand was dialing.

Night of the Klan, A Reporter's Story

It was nearly midnight by now. Claudette and I turned out the lights and took turns the rest of the night waiting and watching out the windows. There was seldom any traffic late at night on our small residential street. That night about the only vehicle I saw go by was one marked Franklin Police Department and driven by Sgt. Shepherd. It made me feel a little better.

Trouble came at the first light of dawn.

From the window I could see a dark sedan sitting only about ten yards away from the house. The vehicle held two men and it bore what looked to be Michigan license plates. I screamed for Claudette and we collided in the hallway.

"Oh God," I muttered racing for the telephone, "Its them. Its the Klan."

The special telephone number the FBI agent had given me must have been a very good one because it was answered almost immediately. Gasping I told the agent about the car outside and the two men in it.

"It's okay," the agent said at last. "They're our people."

I thanked the nice FBI agent and weakly hung up the phone. Claudette and I hugged and kissed in the silence.

At least the night was over.

DAYBREAK

chapter 7

For the next two days nothing happened. Sunday came and went without incident. Monday, the Labor Day holiday was equally uneventful. We watched and waited without leaving home. The telephone never rang. Looking down the street from time to time we occasionally saw strange cars lingering in the vicinity but usually they didn't stay very long. Other vehicles would pass by the house but it was really impossible to know if their route had anything to do with us. A pick-up truck slowly driving by could have been Klu Klux 'wrecking crew' or it could have been three guys just on the way to their favorite fishing spot.

Not only did telephone calls not come in during those two days we also tried to avoid calling out, just in case the prosecutor, police, or FBI might attempt to contact us. During the afternoon on Labor Day I did break our telephone silence to call fellow Daily Journal reporter Dan Logsdon who I knew would be home. Dan was a good friend as well as a good reporter who worked closely with me. Eventually Dan's talent at investigative reporting and attention to detail would take him on to a career as chief detective for the white-collar crime division of the Indiana State Police. But in the early September days of 1969 he was simply a very good journalist. He knew that I had been covering the Klan for sometime, but he was more than a little surprised as I recounted to him on the telephone the details of the previous Saturday evening.

"Damn," he said at last, "you'd better keep your door locked."

I told Dan that I was preparing a written statement of what happened, all the details, for the prosecutor's office. Beyond that I explained I wanted him to handle coverage of any developments on the story. Now that Claudette and I were victims of a crime, the professional role of covering it for the newspaper had to belong to someone else. Dan was well qualified for the task. Despite the fact that it was a holiday, I knew Dan would immediately be making contacts on the story. Logsdon was just that kind of dedicated journalist.

Claudette and I spent much of the remaining holiday trying to figure out what we would have to face in the days immediately ahead. While I had a good deal of experience covering the criminal justice system, the role of being the victim of a serious crime was completely foreign. At least it had been until a few short days ago. Our major concern at this point was the impact of all these events on our two children and the possible dangers that would follow. Matthew could stay with his mother at home, but Judith was enrolled in kindergarten at nearby Webb Elementary school.

Claudette said she would personally take Judith to kindergarten the following school day on Tuesday. The one person she was sure would never be part of any Klan conspiracy would be the kindergarten teacher at Webb. Gladys Glover was African-American. As paranoid as it may sound today, at the time we suddenly were just not that sure about most everybody else. If they were not direct Klan members, maybe they were 'shadow' Klan, or at least very sympathetic to the KKK cause. Very early on the morning of Tuesday, September 2, 1969, I peered out the front window and found a very tranquil scene. No strange cars, no robed Klansmen, not even a barking dog. I unlocked the front door and cautiously edged it open. No one was there. Good.

Just as I was easing the door shut again, my eye caught a small white paper somehow stuck into the frame of the screen door. I reached around the door's edge and grabbed it with my thumb and finger. It was a crisp business card. In bold black letters it read:

"You have just been visited by the Knights of the Klu Klux Klan."

Bastards, I muttered myself, ripping up the card and stuffing the pieces in the pocket of my robe. Our so-called security had apparently been breached. At least it wasn't a bomb. Not this time anyway. I decided not to mention the Klan calling card to Claudette for now. About twenty minutes later I kissed Claudette and the kids goodbye and headed for the newspaper office. Logsdon was at his desk when I arrived. He had already made some calls, but so far the state police had nothing official on the incident. Meanwhile the prosecutor was due in his office soon and Logsdon would be dropping by there. I handed Dan my typed three-page statement of what had transpired the previous Saturday evening, and suggested he make a copy of it before giving the original to the prosecutor. For the next few hours I went about my duties as news editor of the daily newspaper. In our operation at least the news editor, sometimes called the managing editor, had total responsibility for the daily production. The actual editor mostly wrote editorials and represented the newspaper socially in the Johnson County community.

The Daily Journal editor in chief arrived around 9 a.m. on that day but didn't seem all that concerned about my account of the Klan story. I told him Logsdon was on the story. The editor left about ten minutes later for the coffee shop.

Dan Logsdon was back by mid-morning with the makings of a pretty good news story. Prosecutor Joe VanValer had read my statement, heard from his deputy Terence Eads, and was saying for the record that the case was under investigation. Moreover Logsdon had my notes of activities that had gone on during the rally. Perhaps best of all he had prints, developed in the Daily Journal darkroom, from the roll of film Claudette had 'smuggled' out of the rally. The prints were not great but they did show activity at the Klan rally.

By our noon deadline, Logsdon had filed the initial Klan story and was on the telephone to the Indianapolis bureau of the United Press International news service. The Journal subscribed to the UPI wire service, and under a mutual agreement the newspaper was obliged to offer up any major breaking stories in our coverage area once our deadline had been met. The UPI bureau of course could use whatever part of the story they wanted, or not use it at all, depending on the importance of it.

The Daily Journal went to press with the Klan story that day, the story included the prosecutor's promise to investigate, and my own personal narrative of it. By mid-afternoon the wires of United Press International were moving the reporter-at-Klan-gunpoint story too. In the journalistic parlance of the time they had given it a 'good ride' meaning fairly prominent coverage. At this point the Klan story was no longer local. Newspapers, radio stations, and television stations most everywhere would be taking a look at it. Even the film 'smuggling' aspect of it was out. United Press International concluded their story by noting:

"The Daily Journal used pictures of the rally in its Tuesday editions from a roll Reed had saved before the camera was taken."

Well, actually Claudette had saved it, I said to myself as I read the yellow strip of copy paper humming through the UPI teletype printer.

What I was reading on the United Press International teleprinter was also being read by personnel of the Federal Bureau of Investigation in Washington, D.C. Their own UPI teleprinter fed by neatly boxed stacks of white newsprint-like paper similar to the yellow paper I had read, rapidly recorded the news story which had been picked-up by the news service to run on their major A-wire. At FBI headquarters the original and three copies came off of the machine at the same time. Specialists monitored the information and put check marks by news stories that appeared to be of interest to FBI Director John Edgar Hoover.

FBI specialists particularly looked for any items directly mentioning the director himself or operations of the FBI. They also monitored cases under the investigation by the Bureau in general, as well as items pertaining to the Ku Klux Klan that was very much a part of on going FBI investigations. Certain other significant news events as transmitted by United Press International were also noted. At the busy FBI headquarters on a regular workday the original UPI transmissions were clipped, mounted, and routed directly to the Director's Office without background notes. The remaining copies were routed to various ranking officers in the agency. Every seven

Night of the Klan, A Reporter's Story

minutes a messenger picked up the UPI originals and the copies from the Teletype Unit, along with other materials from various other teletypes, and delivered them to the designated offices. In the evenings and on Sundays when the Director's Office was closed, the UPI originals were held in the Teletype Unit until the next morning. Copies of the UPI accounts, when transmitted during non-regular hours were delivered to a designated night duty agent in the Special Investigative Division. However after 7:15 p.m. on workdays and on Sundays most of the UPI copies are held for delivery the following morning.

The reporter-at-Klan-gunpoint story from the wires of United Press International was distributed to various FBI offices late that afternoon. It would be re-distributed early the next day when both UPI and the Associated Press carried up dated accounts of the incident and details of the earlier events. At some point FBI officials in Washington were in touch with agents in the Indianapolis bureau to request further information and to request any intelligence data as to what the reaction within the Klan organization might be. Back in Johnson County, Indiana that afternoon, state police detective Richard Bumps had contacted the county prosecutor's office to ask if the prosecutor needed assistance from the Indiana State Police in regard to the armed robbery of Robert Reed by a security guard of the Ku Klux Klan. (Although Bumps was a friend, I had not yet talked to him about the incident. I felt too that Trooper Ackerman probably had not made a report on the armed robber. So I assumed Logsdon's questions to post headquarters earlier in the day had raised further questions.)

At any rate, prosecutor VanValer concluded at some point during that afternoon that some serious criminal activity had indeed taken place. VanValer related to detective Bumps that he planned to seek a criminal arrest warrant on the chief of security of the Indiana Klux Klan. Bumps immediately contracted the Intelligence Section of the Indiana State Police and learned that the KKK chief of security was specifically indeed a person named Joe Napier, a resident of Indianapolis. The State Police I.S. provided Bumps with Napier's home address. Later in the afternoon VanValer telephoned me at the newspaper office with an update on his investigation. He added that Detective Bumps was a part of the investigation.

"We've asked for a probable court hearing in the morning in Johnson Circuit court," the prosecutor told me. "You need to be there to answer some questions for us. You'll have to testify under oath."

VanValer further suggested that if the Klan guard was arrested I may also have to identify him in a police lineup.

"Can you do that for us?"

I said yes because I was sure I would recognize the only person in the world who had ever threatened me at gunpoint. But another part of me wanted to say no, because I really wasn't up to seeing that Klan guard face-to-face again. Back at home, Claudette reported that Mrs. Glover fully understood the situation and would be watchful. She told us to be careful too. That evening Klan security chief Joe Napier received a telephone call alerting him that a John Doe warrant was being prepared seeking his arrest for armed robbery. Although Napier did later admit that the night call had tipped him off, police never learned who had actually made the call to the Klansman that night.

At about the same time that Napier was receiving his call, Grand Dragon Chaney was releasing a hurried statement to the news media, He said he had first learned of the incident when an Indianapolis newspaper reporter has called about 6 P.M. that evening. Chaney told reporters he always thought Reed gave the KKK "fair Coverage", and although he didn't always agree with the newspaper he "respected the job Reed did." Chaney confirmed, in his brief statement, that he had repeatedly announced at the Klan rally, reporters were welcome to take pictures.

"One reporter took a picture and the Klansmen resented it, but I told them, don't think anything of it, these reporters are our guests," Chaney added.

The Grand Dragon then went on to "publicly apologize," and further that the Klan person involved would be "called upon the carpet. No one should flash guns around." He concluded his comments that evening by saying, "I carry a gun in the car myself, But I don't approve of flashing them around."

Later that same evening I received a telephone call at home.

"You'd better not be at that hearing tomorrow," said a husky male voice. "Ya hear me?"

The phone clicked silent.

I had heard.

Night of the Klan, A Reporter's Story

HIGH NOON

chapter 8

Any idle hope that the Klan would let one of their own go to jail without making every effort to prevent it, whatever it might take, had vanished with that anonymous telephone call. The earlier KKK calling card told me they could reach right to our front door if they really, really, wanted to reach it. The late night call told me they weren't hesitant to make direct threats even when the FBI, State Police, and prosecutor were all involved in the investigation. Okay. Make the call.

The Indiana State police post said Detective Bumps was not there but if the matter was urgent they would try and get a message to him. I stressed the urgent part and left my name and number. Bumps returned my call within 15 minutes.

He sounded annoyingly cheerful on the phone, "So what's happening? Has the Klan put you on their Klabogal list?"

"No so funny Bumps," I told him about the card and more importantly and just as quickly about the threat in the telephone call. My tone was hushed and serious. And his tone changed abruptly.

"Bob, we can get a (state police) car there if necessary. Take you right up to the courthouse steps and all," he said.

I wasn't buying. "No, I think these guys are serious. And this is getting...well, getting to be too much. Let's forget it."

"You mean the threat", Bumps asked.

"No, I mean the whole damned thing. Forget the hearing. I got my family not to mention myself to consider. Klan one, me zero. Klan wins. Game over."

Detective Bumps took a deep breath.

"Look Bob, you know better than that. A conviction here could put them on the run, cost them money, cause bickering within the ranks. Don't scare out on this."

Scare out? Oh yes. Says so right here across my shirt.

In the next few minutes, despite myself, Detective Bumps had talked me right back into the courtroom. I agreed reluctantly to be at the next morning's probable cause hearing at the Johnson County courthouse. Maybe no one would really notice.

While I tried fitfully to sleep, the Associated Press was moving this updated story on their overnight wires for morning news outlets:

Robert M. Reed

"Franklin, Ind. (AP) Warrants will be sought today for the arrest of a Klu Klux Klan security guard who allegedly threatened the life of a reporter and seized his camera at a Klan rally Saturday night.

Joe VanValer, prosecutor of Brown and Johnson counties said a probable cause hearing will today seek to determine if there is sufficient evidence to issue warrants charging robbery and commission of a felony while armed.

"VanValer said the guard had not been identified but police have a suspect.

"Reed reported that the guard wore a type of military uniform, was not hooded and could be identified by him.

He said Indiana Grand Dragon William Chaney, presiding over the rally, announced from the platform, "You newspapermen are our guests and can do anything you wish—just like in your own backyard."

"About 100 persons attended the rally and cross burning on a farm near Samaria in Brown County."

Wednesday morning, at exactly 9 a.m. I walked alone up the courthouse steps and into the Johnson Circuit courtroom. Prosecutor VanValer and deputy prosecutor Eads were waiting. Otherwise the enormous Victorian-era courtroom was empty. Presently we were joined by judge Robert Young. Around the courthouse Judge Young, distinguished and graying, could be quite cordial and kindly. In the courtroom he was quite intent and serious. When the judge had been seated, I was told to take the witness stand.

The prosecutor began with a few preliminary questions about my name and address and then went immediately to the Klan rally in Brown County.

Q—"Now directing your attention to the dusk of that day or thereabouts, later afternoon or early evening, did you have an occasion to be in your automobile with your wife?"

A—"Yes, I did.

Q—"Would you tell the court what happened briefly in your words as you were leaving and taking a photograph?

A—"As we were leaving I had my camera and attempted to take a picture of a man armed with a rifle. We sat in the car with the motor running and he came up to the car rather quickly, and put the rifle through the window. And he said, "I told you not to take my picture." And I explained to him that Chaney in charge of the group, had given me permission to take pictures. Then he put the gun at my head and said he was gonna blow my head off. And he repeated the statement and said, "You hear what I said, didn't you?" Then he demanded the film from the camera and before I could unload the camera he un-grabbed the camera itself, while he still had the gun at my head, and told me to get out of there and if he ever saw me again he'd kill me. So we left.

Night of the Klan, A Reporter's Story

Q—"He did take the camera from you?
A—"Yes, camera, flash attachment and the film, of course that was in the camera.
Q—"And were you in fear when that happened?
A—"Yes, I was.

There were other questions as to my ability to identify the Klan guard. I described his uniform, his weapon, and the fact that he identified himself as Chief of Security. The prosecutor also asked about the invitation letter I had received earlier at the newspaper office.

Q—"In any of that literature was there any reference to who the Chief of Security was?
A—"The Chief of Security according to the letter was identified as Joe Napier."
Q—"I believe you testified here already that there was a rifle?
A—"Right.
Q—"And did you have occasion earlier than this to observe that the rifle or other rifles being loaded with live ammunition?
A—"Yes, as we arrived at the rally we were in the parking area. Immediately in front of us was this same man and another man who were loading rifles from ammunition in the trunk of a car. We observed that as we entered.

At this point in the probable cause hearing, Judge Young had a few questions of his own.

Q— "Do you think you can identify the man who—-
A— "Yes, I think so. He was within in a rifle barrel distance.
Q— "How long did this take for the whole thing to take place?
A—"I suppose about five minutes totally.
Q—"Who was with you?
A—"My wife was with me in the car."

The prosecutor then addressed a few more questions as I continued on the witness stand.

Q—"Did you have an occasion to observe this man earlier in the day?
A—"Yes, we were at the meeting, this rally for about two hours. And we saw this same man off and on the whole time.
Q—"So you had a period of time longer than what was encompassed (the five minutes) in this particular act to—
A—"Right, it was the same person. We saw him loading the rifle and then we observed him the two hours that we were there at the rally."

Judge Young turned to me with a few more questions.

Q—"And he was carrying a rifle during that time?
A—"Yes sir.
Q—"And they haven't returned your camera?

A—"Uh, after we left the scene we flagged down a State Trooper who was in a patrol car and uh- I told him what had happened and he said that he would see if he would get the camera back. And he left the scene and he returned in about 15 minutes later and had the camera, although the film had been torn out."

Both the judge and the prosecutor thanked me. The probable cause hearing ended about 20 minutes after it began. In the hallway VanValer said they would be in touch with me later in the day.

Outside the courtroom a few people had gathered to await the court's ruling and see how the local reporter was holding up under the growing ordeal. The first to shake my hand was seasoned Franklin attorney James D. Acher. Acher was a former prosecutor, and at that time the dean of just about all that was judicial in the community.

"Young man," he said with a smile, "those Klan guys really do mean business." Acher, who walked haltingly with a cane, had been around long enough to remember the Klu Klux Klan of the 1920s.

Without waiting for a response he leaded forward, bracing himself on his cane, and said quietly, "If I were you son, I'd start wearing a hog leg on your side."

"What," I asked, "is a hog leg?"

"Its a gun," he said patting my shoulder, "its a gun."

By the time I had left the courthouse and driven the few miles to the Daily Journal newspaper office there were several pink slip messages waiting for me. A good many newspaper reporters, editors, publishers, and just good citizens had called to offer encouragement and well wishes. There was also a message from the prosecutor's office advising me to be at the Greenwood police department at 1 p.m. for the line up. Authorities expected to have the suspect in custody by that time according to the message.

While my stomach was ruling out any thought of lunch, Detective Richard Bumps and Sgt. Gary McPherson of the Indiana State Police were serving the warrants on Klan guard Joe Napier at his residence in Indianapolis. Napier offered no resistance, and was taken by police patrol car to Greenwood.

VanValer met me outside the Greenwood Police station and said the lineup would be held next door in the Greenwood City Court Room. The prosecutor explained that there would be six white males in the line up, all of them more or less the same age range and with a similar body build as the suspect. I was to carefully view the line up and then write down the number of the position in which the person whom I believed to be the suspect was standing.

Inside the brightly lit courtroom I was seated at a small wooden table. The prosecutor gave me a slip of paper with six numbers on it. I was to circle one. The six people were brought into the room and stood facing me about 15 feet away.

I was nervous but I spotted the Klan guard right away. The six men did look somewhat similar, just as the prosecutor had said, but there was no doubt. Each man in the line up was asked to step forward and say in a normal voice:

"You remember what I said, don't you. Don't you."

Then in a loud voice each said:

"I'm going to blow your head off."

This done, the prosecutor handed me a pencil and I circled the number. I was removed from the room briefly, and when I was returned the six were still standing there in the same line but in a different order.

They went through the same vocal procedure again. And again I was given a paper with numbers. In circled the number of the position where the Klan guard stood.

Outside prosecutor VanValer thanked me for being there.

"I know you were scared," he said, "that's just what crime victims have to go through."

"But was I..."

VanValer nodded, "You picked the Klan's chief of security both times."

While I was driving back to Franklin, state police officer McPherson and deputy prosecutor Eads were taking a statement from the suspect.

The official summary of statement by defendant Joe Napier, September 3, 1969 was as follows:

"The meeting was held after line-up and finger printing and mugging (photographing) of the defendant, just before his transportation to the Brown County Jail. Before any questions were asked, the charges and what had transpired up to that time were explained to the defendant. Next, he was advised of his constitutional rights.

"Then, pursuant to question and answer, the following information was disclosed by the defendant:

"He is a member of an organization known as the Knights of the Klu Klux Klan. That organization held and sponsored the meeting in Brown County on Saturday night, August 29, on a farm sought of Spearsville, Indiana. He was present at that meeting.

"He is Chief of Security for said organization for this area. He had been Chief of Security for a couple of weeks; he was not certain of the exact length of time, but his appointment was published in the local newspaper here.

"He was in the gray uniform along with three other security guards in gray uniforms, which were under his direction. There were other guards there in dark uniforms; they were from another area, but he does not know where. He was not carrying a rifle that evening nor were any of the other three men carrying a rifle or armed to the best of his knowledge, because if he had known about it, he would have not allowed it.

"He had no insignia or other badge on his uniform to distinguish him as Chief of Security. He and the other three security officers did have a gold leaf decoration. The other three wore it on their arms, he wore his on the collar. He thinks that the other three security officers had on black ties, but he had on a white tie.

"He does not know Bob Reed and does not remember seeing Bob Reed at the meeting, but thinks he knows which one he was, if he was the newspaper man with the green suit or green outfit of some sort.

"He was not present at the alleged scene of this crime when it allegedly took place and the first knowledge that he had that this had even occurred was the night before he was arrested when he received a telephone call.

"He refused to give the names of the other three security guards who were at the meeting, because such would be in violation of his oath and obligation to the KKK, because by doing so he would in effect be stating that someone else was a member of that organization.

"He did not recall that anyone took a picture of him that evening although he might be in a picture, because as the people at the meeting were proceeding in a line to the cross burning, he was standing in the area and he thought that this person in green clothes was taking pictures of them; therefore, he might be in one of those pictures.

"The area for parking cars was across the road from the area in which the meeting was held. He stayed at the area of the meeting all night and was with his wife. He was never down in the area of the parked cars until he was ready to leave and at that time he only recalls about three cars that were left in the parking area, one of which he thought belonged to Chaney.

"To the best of his knowledge, no one was armed with a rifle at the meeting. The only person he saw with a rifle was a man off in the distance when he first arrived which he assumed was a hunter, but he has no idea who he was. He did not appear to be present at the meeting."

Napier did disclose further to authorities that afternoon that he currently owned three high powered rifles including a Russian-made .30 caliber rifle and a British Enfield bolt action rifle. Many years later FBI informant Gary Rowe would note in writing of his latter 1960s undercover years with the Ku Klux Klan, that to correct the "weapon deficiency" in many KKK units a great volume of British Enfield rifles were introduced. Purchased in large numbers through surplus stores, they were offered "at each meeting in raffles or given as prizes. I would estimate that the Klan had 3,000 or more of these rifles." Indiana, Alabama, and many of states in between did not require a permit for rifles of this nature.

Night of the Klan, A Reporter's Story

Detective Bumps and Sgt. McPherson drove the Klan guard from the Greenwood Police Station to the Brown County jail in Nashville. Another state police unit with two other officers followed behind them. During the ride the two officers offered to make arrangements for a lie detector test for Napier. Napier declined, and said nothing more during the trip.

If Napier wasn't talking about the Klan incident, he was just about the only one.

By about 4 p.m. that day the Franklin Evening Star, our newspaper competition, was on the streets with its Wednesday edition. A heavy black Bulletin notice headed a column on the front page. It read:

"BULLETIN

Johnson Circuit court Judge Robert Young late this morning issued a warrant for the arrest of Joe Napier, security chief for the Indiana Klu Klux Klan. Napier is charged with armed robbery and is to be arrested by officials of the Brown County Sheriff's office.

Judge Young set bond at $20,000. Napier is charged with the assault and robbery of Franklin newsman Robert M. Reed, 60 N. Middleton Drive."

Meanwhile at the Brown County jail Napier was booked and finger printed by Indiana state trooper Stewart Smith and placed in a cell. At the booking process a scale determined his weight to be 170 pounds and a wall chart put his height at 5 feet and 11 inches. Much earlier in that long day, at the probable cause hearing I had described him as 180 pounds and maybe six feet tall. However I had estimated his age at 35, and he was actually 43 years of age. At nightfall Grand Dragon William Chaney and about a dozen Klansmen appeared immediately outside the Brown County jail. Brown County deputy sheriff Wayne Branham, alerted that there may be trouble, met them at the front door of the jail.

Deputy Branham recalled later than Chaney had demanded to see inmate Napier to "see if the accused man was their Joe." The deputy sheriff calmly told the band that visiting hours were over for the day. The deputy said that even with posting bond that no releases and no visitors were permitted after 5:30 p.m. each day. Chaney said he and the others would return the following morning.

By Thursday morning I was in the center of a whirlwind of news coverage, which obviously is about the worst place that a journalist could ever be. The Indianapolis Star and other morning newspapers around the state fueled by the arrest of the Klan guard gave the story major play. On the news wires the Klan story lead the bureau 'breaks' on both Associated Press and United Press International. More people called the office. Congressman Lee Hamilton's office telephoned their support and interest, as did an assistant to United States Senator Birch Bayh. In the midst of the clamor Detective Bumps called to check on the state's "major witness." Bumps said

89

Robert M. Reed

they expected Napier to soon be released on bond from the Brown County jail but the Klan was having trouble raising the money. I asked the detective if all this media publicity would irritate the Klan further. Bumps admitted candidly it probably didn't help the situation much.

"You've drawn a hell of lot of attention to them," he said, "and that in turn is making it a big issue with the Klan. They have to be pretty uncomfortable by now."

While I was still on the phone with Bumps, two FBI agents walked into the office and flashed their impressive credentials. We went directly to the small conference room where they asked questions for about an hour. I was in the mood to offer up just about every detail I had accumulated so far on the Klan including right down to their robe sizes. (Chaney wore a large.) They were pleasant enough but not all that reassuring.

Some of the Klan, said the two agents, "are capable of just about anything."

They instructed me to use caution in the days ahead. Keep my car as secure as possible, not to use the same routine routes to and from work, and avoid being out alone at night. At least for a while. What they declined to specifically state was just how dangerous they considered some members of the Ku Klu Klan to really be. Their own confidential memos had long since notified regional offices of the Bureau "that since members have been known to carry concealed weapons, they should be considered armed and dangerous." As we sat at the conference table they glanced at one another but did not tell me that part. Given everything else that had already happened I would then likely have ran all the way home-had they disclosed that part. Wise FBI agents these two guys. In the end they did however assure me that they would be using FBI resources to prevent any KKK violence aimed at myself or my family. The Indiana State Police had said pretty much the same thing. Even the local police had tried, in their way, to be assuring. I remained plainly and unconditionally afraid.

Later that same Thursday the Franklin Evening Star carried still another front page story. Headlined, Reed Given Guard, it read in part:

"A protective ring of security was placed about a Franklin newsman, his family and his home today, following the arrest of an Indiana Ku Klux Klan security guard for allegedly threatening the life of the newsman.

"Police reported a security force is on duty to protect newsman Robert Reed and his family, 60 Middleton Drive, Franklin.

"The guard was ordered following the arrest of an Indianapolis man, reportedly the chief of a Klan security force who was on duty at a KKK rally in Brown County Saturday."

It went on to give an account of much of what somehow which had transpired in the past six days.

Night of the Klan, A Reporter's Story

I glanced at the headline again and shuddered.

ANOTHER DAY

chapter 9

By Friday morning the situation remained uneasy and unpredictable. Claudette and I had barricaded the front door again the night before, and kept the outside light burning. I drove to work on what I considered to be an 'alternative route' and attempted to be wary of any strange vehicles behind me. At the newspaper office maintaining the routine was also difficult. Most everyone at the Daily Journal was concerned about the business with the Ku Klux Klan and they were supportive, but still it was distracting to the daily news operation. Messages and telephone still came in regarding the stand-down with the Klan. Even a few copies of editorials in out-of-town newspapers had landed on my desk.

In Bloomington, Indiana the Courier-Tribune observed, "newsman Reed is not happy or satisfied with the outcome. His story was picked up by the wire services, radio stations and a television network...he's not resting easily these days...It is a story of fear and courage."

In Nashville, Indiana The Brown County Democrat ran a front page editorial decrying the event which had transpired right in their own backyard. The editorial blasted, "the Ku Klux Klan or any organization that would take the law into its own hands; that would have a public meeting with guards armed with guns where there was not a threat to the peace or security of a community; that would threatened the life and freedom of an individual on a public highway, steal his camera and confiscate film."

At my newspaper, The Daily Journal, an editorial the day before had been a little less bold. It proclaimed, "given the facts it is our opinion that people will ultimately make the right decision, whether such a decision involves the Klan or anything else."

Logsdon and others on the staff agreed that the hapless editor just did not fully understand the situation with the Klan. On Friday morning, when he arrived in the office, the editor called me over to make one of his very few comments on a Klan story that was running on the front page of the majority of newspapers in the Midwest. He was concerned about the windows. The landmark Daily Journal building was largely a glass structure and the editor was concerned that an angry band of Klansman might seek their revenge on the building.

"We don't want them getting mad and then coming out here and busting the windows," he grimly told me.

Night of the Klan, A Reporter's Story

I wanted to mention that the Klan was probably already pretty angry at me and at the newspaper, but I kept my mouth shut. I also decided to decline seeking any advice on exactly how we would keep the Klan from 'getting mad' in the future. I deeply hoped he did not mean to imply that I should walk away from the criminal case. Fortunately the editor was anxious to leave for the coffee shop, and the conversation ended. I decided not to worry too much about the Journals windows.

The Klan guard remained in the Brown County jail that Friday still under $20,000 bond. According to sources Napier was not commenting on the charges or on any Klan related matters. Thus far the Klan organization had either been unable or unwilling to post bond for their security guard. Over the next few days there were rumors than the KKK was in quandary over current developments in Indiana. Chaney and some others in the Klan were "passing the hat" among members and calling for further contributions to the Defense Fund.

The KKK needed finances not only to defend Napier, but also to mount a defense in court for Chaney and the others who had been arrested with hundreds of pounds of dynamite. Both of the legal courses would be expensive. Informants had whispered to authorities that more than one Klansman had suggested taking other measures to win the release of the Klan guard. My source, Detective Bumps, did not go into any details as to the "other measures" other than to say all of them were unpleasant.

On the following Monday morning the two FBI agents who had appeared in the newspaper office on the previous Thursday were back at the Daily Journal. In the conference room they passed around actual photographs and newspaper clipping photographs to see if I recognized any people. Most of the images were of Klansmen at various public events taken by various means over the year. Some of the Klan I knew, having seen them before, and others I was not familiar with. We also covered much of what I told them earlier, and they wondered if I had any contact with the Klan since that time. I told the agents about the telephone call warning, and the KKK card I had found in the doorframe. – it was the only information I had omitted in our first 'interview' session. They again cautioned me to be watchful and to alert them if I was threatened.

Seeing the FBI's collection of Klan character photographs got me curious and as soon as they left I began searching through my own rather bulky Klan files. Eventually I found what I was searching for. It was a contact sheet of negatives from a roll of film of Klan security guards that I had taken at one of their private meetings. We had never published this particular photograph but the sheet had a file date on the back. I asked the darkroom technician to pull the negatives from that file date to see if we could come up with a decent print of it. About twenty minutes later I had a

Robert M. Reed

full-sized black and white print of four Klan security guards complete with helmets and uniforms. One of the four was Joe Napier.

That afternoon at the Brown Circuit Court the joint Brown-Johnson Circuit Court judge Robert Young reduced the Klan guard's bond from $20,000 to $5,000—-$2,500 each for the two criminal charges. Napier, with his defense attorney Michael Dugan II of Indianapolis, asked that his arraignment on the charges (where he would be required to enter a plea of guilty or not guilty) be continued. As was court routine, the request for a delay in the arraignment process was granted. Shortly afterwards two Brown County residents posted a property bond to free Napier. The property involved was the "old Zimmerman farm" where the KKK rally had taken place. It was described a being about two miles north of Fox's Corner on the Spearsville Road. Under the conditions of a property bond court authorities hold the deed to the property until proceedings against the defendant conclude. The Klan organization itself, for whatever reasons, had not come up with the bond finances.

Detective Bumps called me at the office to alert me to the fact that Napier was now out of jail. I told him about the newly discovered photograph and said he would pass along the information to the prosecutor's office. Not surprisingly someone from the prosecutor's office called the first thing Tuesday morning and asked if I could come there that afternoon to give a deposition on the case. I took the photograph with me. The prosecutor had some photographs of his own. Many of the photographs were quite similar to those I had seen the day before in the possession of the FBI agents. I assumed they had also visited the prosecutor's office.

The first questions however were about the photograph I had brought with me.

Q. "Please feel free to make any comment on the photograph if you have any.

A. "This is the picture of the same person that was present at the Klan meeting with the rifle.

Q. "You are referring to the Klan meeting.

A. "One of two men.

Q "When you say Klan meeting, are you referring to the Klan meeting which took place in Brown County a week ago Saturday?

A. "That's correct."

Q. "Can you indicate on that picture which man you are talking about?

A. "Its the man on the right. There are four men. The one on the right."

Q. "Now is there anything else?

A "Well the uniform and the dress is almost exactly the one he had on at that time.

Q. "And the photograph has four people dressed in Klan security uniforms?

A. "That's correct.

Q. "Now is this the same man on the far right as you referred to as Napier—is that the same man that you picked out of the line-up last Wednesday at the Greenwood Police Department?

A. "That's correct.

Q. "Would you be able to identify the if you saw him...the other security guard that you have referred to as at the meeting...the Saturday meeting in Brown County?

A. "I believe so."

And we continued sorting and identifying photographs as I gave me testimony. Eventually we came to a newspaper photograph from a Spencer, Indiana newspaper showing two Klansmen in robes beside two Klan guards in full uniform holding bolt action rifles. The rifles appeared to be identical.

Q. "Now we have a picture of four people, two security guards and two robed individuals, is that correct?

A. "Yes.

Q. "Which one of the men in there looks to be the second security guard at the Brown County rally?

A. "It would be the second one from the left.

The questioning continued on for some time exploring the details of my description of both Napier and the other Klan guard and their weapons.

A. "Napier and the other guard both carried rifles. There were two or three others that had dark blue shirts, but similar dress who were present at my car at that time.

Q. "I see, did they also have weapons?

A. "One of the other men also had a rifle. There were three rifles in all counting the one that was at my head. They all seemed to be exactly the same.

Q. "What do you mean when you say they all seemed to be exactly the same?

A. "The rifles appeared to be exactly the same make and so forth.

Q. "How much do you know about rifles?

A. "Not a great deal.

Q "You are not a gun collector?

A "I am not too familiar with firearms, but I did have occasion as my wife and I arrived at the scene to see these same men loading these same rifles.

Q. "Did you happen to notice whether these were bolt action weapons or pump action weapons?

"A. They appeared to be bolt action weapons.

When the session ended, VanValer noted that Klan guard who I had identified in the newspaper photo of guards and robed Klansman was Gary D Richardson.

That evening as Claudette and I sat at home we received another haunting telephone call.

"Look here Reed," said the same husky male voice that had been on the phone the night before the probable cause hearing, "we know you been talkin' to that prosecutor again. You end it or we will."

Then the line was dead. That night Claudette and I once again moved the furniture across the front door. I wondered if this routine would eventually develop our upper body muscles. I decided not to call authorities this time. It hadn't helped before.

The September days went by without any further incident, Claudette and gradually went about the routine of our lives. We were wary, especially if we drove anywhere with the children, but we assured ourselves with the fact that nothing serious had happened so far. As the story slipped from nearly day to day coverage, so had the attention it generated. Some older citizens, who remembered the D.C. Stephenson's Klan of the Roaring Twenties far too fondly, wondered what all the fuss about with myself and the current Klan. Most of the community totally distained both the old and the new Ku Klux Klan. There were a few exceptions. The anonymous phone calls had ceased as the month dwindled. This could have been because I had not been involved in any further court proceedings in the case since the question and answer session in the prosecutor's office. Or it could have been because the Klan had more or less lost interest. I was hoping for the latter.

Against some good advice I ended up, a few days later, working into the evening at the newspaper office. The Daily Journal building was constructed six years earlier in 1963, in part to be a showplace. And it was. The unique building stood on a knoll on the northern outskirts of Franklin just off of US Highway 31. At the time its nearly all-glass construction was a startling sight. The intent of the architect was to create, among other things, a vast visual openness for passing motorists. During the day the view was impressive. All the typical activity associated with a daily newspaper including the huge press could be seen through the giant glass walls that extended from floor to ceiling.

'At night, if anything, the building was even more impressive. From the outside it was cascaded with super flood lights which gave the glass itself and the stark white framing which surrounded it an enriching glow. Since much of the remaining property remained either undeveloped or at relatively unlit and dark at night, the Daily Journal building could be seen literally for miles. For all of its activity during the day, the mighty newspaper building was just as deserted during the evening. In 1969 the people who labored at advertising, composition, printing, reporting, and the other relative operations of the day were usually glad to be away from the structure at night. Later the newspaper and other production would turn the building into a near 24-hour operation, but that particular September it remained simply a brightly lit but very empty building.

My plan had been to work at the office awhile since I would more than likely be away the following morning for some court procedure involving the Klan guard case. The prosecutor's office had indicated that I may not be needed at all, but to plan on being away for the morning anyway. Even at this relatively early stage of the court proceedings I inwardly dreaded appearing in court and then once again going through all the chilling details of being held at gunpoint. It was never a pleasant experience.-

Most all of the law enforcement people I had come into contact with in the days that followed the armed robbery and arrest of the Klan guard had urged personal caution on my part. None them had said to forever barricade myself and family in the house, but then too they didn't suggest sitting in such a highly visible building in the dark of night either. I didn't plan to stay at the Journal office long. Claudette and the kids were safe at home. For some reason, never fully explained, the prosecutor's office had entirely held off from yet involving Claudette in any of the criminal justice proceedings. Earlier that night I had asked my brother to stop the house and keep the family company until I was finished at The Daily Journal. Sitting alone at my desk I abruptly heard the parking lot doors of the building jar to a close. For all of its perfection, the glass walls always gave a slight shutter whenever the heavy doors opening into the parking lot slammed shut. For a daffy instant I thought perhaps my brother had decided to come by the office after stopping at the house. I was wrong.

My desk faced the brightly lit windows of the building, the dark entrance hallway was just off behind me. I heard footsteps and turned to look into the face of Grand Dragon William Chaney and another Klansman at his side. This was the first encounter, other than the anonymous telephone calls, with any of the Klan since the whole episode in the wilds of Brown County. I leapt up but my feet but they couldn't seem to make up their mine to run or to stand. My hands trembled.

"We were just in the neighborhood," said Chaney smiling but never lifting his eyes away from mine.

Chaney then introduced the Klansman standing next to him. They were wearing street clothes of course, and not robes. But they might as well have been wearing robes. Part of my frightened mind was seeing the two of them standing there in those damned Klan robes. The 'new' security chief smiled at me and deftly undid the button of his plaid sports coat. It was easy to see he was wearing a handgun. I think the whole point was for me to see the gun. Chaney, who privately had said he never went anywhere without his gun, kept smiling at me too. I guess I was the lone sourpuss in this crowd.

"So," asked the Klan guard pointedly, "where's your family?"

Oh God no! My mind was reeling. No, no. This is not happening. They have Claudette and the kids. The bastards. Oh no. Suddenly I was more angry than afraid.

"What the hell are you saying?," I shouted. "What are you telling me!"

Chaney and the Klan guard seemed a little taken back. They glanced at one another.

"Ah, you know…where's your family from?" the Klan guard continued. "Ah, you know. Where your people came from."

On yes, that family. Oh sure…relatives.

My great aunt Mary Anderson had lived all her life in Jeffersonville, Indiana. A prodigy as child, she had become a major commercial artist doing renderings of a number of household products for magazine advertisements. One of her most famous contributions had been the Morton Salt Girl. My mother, then seven years old, had been the model for one of the popular "when it rains it pours" images of that era. Great aunt Mary died when I was a child, but I didn't think she would mind if made use of her good name and hometown in such a situation.

"Jeffersonville," I finally stammered to the Klan security chief. "That place is full my relatives."

"Nice town," the Guard nodded knowingly.

There was pause. I remained at my desk obviously uncomfortable. Chaney and his bodyguard prepared to leave.

"I just wanted you to meet him," Chaney said nodding toward the guard. He added flatly, "we'll be a watchin' out for ya."

I was pounding out the number of the Indiana State Police post as the glass walls of the Daily Journal building rumbled the departure of the two into the darkness of the parking lot.

"I need to get an urgent message to Detective Bumps," I excitedly told the answering voice.

Although I had left the Daily Journal telephone number for Bumps to call back, I totally lacked the courage to wait even a few minutes for the return call. I ran from the building and purposefully left all the inside lights burning bright. At least the feet were working again. Inside the car, racing toward home, the old fear was back. Suddenly all of the terror of being held at gunpoint by the Klan was sitting in the seat right beside. Robed Klansmen might just as well have been passengers in the car. Forget all that bringing-bad-guys-to-justice stuff. Forget it. I wanted to be free of it all. I desperately wanted out of whatever I had stumbled into.

Night of the Klan, A Reporter's Story

By the time I reached home on the far-east side of Franklin, the telephone there was ringing. Detective Bumps was returning my call. When I didn't answer at the office, the detective figured I been fleeing home I was. Claudette handed me the phone without comment. Quickly and somewhat breathlessly I told the veteran officer about my Klan visitors.

"You know they are just trying to scare you," Bumps calmly said.

"Well, they did a damn fine job of it. I'm scared," I shouted. In spite of myself my eye were welling with tears. "And to hell with it. Forget this court stuff. Forget me."

I ranted on for a few more minutes.

"Try and settle down, Robert," Bumps said when I was at last finished.

"No super cop. I quit," I said, and softly hung up the phone.

The Klan visit that night did work up to a point. My panic did contribute to the problem. But in the long run the Klan visit backfired. Once the initial fright wore off that night and I again realized whom I was dealing with, I was more determined than ever to see it through to the end. Sheepishly, I called Detective Bumps the next morning and told him I was back in. Bumps said he had faith in me all the time. In those days that was as close to crime victim counseling as it ever got.

Robert M. Reed

ANOTHER NIGHT

chapter 10

By the fall of 1969 the Indiana Realm of the Invisible Empire was having its troubles too.

Klan guard Napier was due back in Brown County court to enter a plea in connection with the charges of robbery and armed robbery. Napier was free on $5,000 bond. Meanwhile Grand Dragon Chaney himself was out on $5,000 bond in connection with his arrest in Monroe County for possession of more than 300 pounds of dynamite. Four of his fellow Klansmen, facing the same charges, were also out of jail on bond. Chaney was also out on bond in connection with his arrest in Michigan on charges of violating a federal firearms act.

Legal fees for all these incidents were rapidly mounting. Klansmen were grumbling about the continued need to finance troubles with the law. They also complained about the great amount of negative national publicity brought about as a result of the gunplay in the Brown County rally. Some of the members privately question the Grand Dragon's leadership and there were whispered rumors about starting a new Klan organization. Interestingly, Gary Richardson, the Klan security guard who had stood shoulder to shoulder with the Chief of Security as they held Claudette and I at gunpoint, was apparently leading the dissenting group within the KKK ranks. By October ex-Klan guard Richardson was one of the leaders of the newly proclaimed Unified Klans of America.

One of Chaney's own Klan loyalists later gave a disposition to the court about the October development.

"We was comin' from a rally on West Washington near Greenfield," the Klan member later testified before the prosecutor, "And we stopped at this truck stop, all of us (Klan members) to get a bite to eat…And I looked over there and the same security guard that took the camera was sittin' over there at a corner table.

"He (Richardson) was identified to me as the head of the Unified Klan of America. Yeah, he had withdrew from the United Klans of America, him and ah a group of rejects. They had their own little deal, and he was referred to me as being the head of it."

At an early point amidst the court dates, Klan turmoil, and telephone threats from unidentified sources, the issue regarding still further protection for my family and myself came up.

Night of the Klan, A Reporter's Story

"Listen," said Detective Bumps, "with all this going on and more ahead you should consider getting yourself a gun. For your protection."

"Oh sure," I broke in, "you mean some kind of a hog leg?"

Bumps smile broadly at the use of the term. Just about everyone I had talked to following the Klan incident thus far especially law enforcement officers had urged me to obtain some sort of weapon. The afternoon after getting Detective Bumps' recommendation as well, I put aside most of my aversions and drove to the Greenwood shopping mall to purchase the first firearm I had ever owned in my life. My choice was a single-action .22 caliber western style pistol with carved wood handle grips. It looked nice and it was on sale. When I showed the purchase the following day to Detective Bumps he seemed amused.

"That's just the gun you need if you're planning on doing a movie soon with Roy Rogers," he chuckled.

After the laughter, Bumps got right now to business. He specifically told me to obtain a .38 caliber handgun, and like it or not—carry it on my person until it could be determined how this Klan thing would unfold.

Carrying the gun, Bumps explained, would require a gun permit. We drove to the Franklin police department for the paper work, and Detective Bumps himself drove to Indiana State Police headquarters to have the application processed. Less than 24 hours later I was licensed to carry a gun I still had not yet purchased. Soon afterwards I acquired a .38 caliber revolver that I never learned to accept. Warnings or not I kept the weapon at home, which turned out to be a bit of a mistake too. If I knew nothing about firearms, Claudette knew somewhat less. A few nights later, while I was away from the house for just a short while, Claudette received still another threatening telephone call vowing, "You'll remember the Klan after tonight." Such calls tended to increase just before a significant court date regarding the earlier summer's armed assault charges.

Terrified, and alone with our two children, Claudette used a chair to reach the handgun where it was kept fully loaded atop the corner cupboard. Hearing noises in the darkness behind the house, and given all that transpired since that dark night in Brown County, she cocked the hammer on the hammer and waited. How long she waited I don't know for sure. She was still there in the kitchen when I finally came home. Claudette held the gun up to me with the hammer still very much cocked and a .38 caliber bullet in the chamber. I took away from her very slowly.

"I didn't know how to work it," she said, her voice softly breaking into sobs.

"I'm sorry," said, hugging her, "I'm sorry about the whole thing." It was a tearful moment for both of us.

Meanwhile the courtroom delays for the criminal processing of the Klan guard continued to mount. The defendant's arraignment was continued twice in October only to be continued twice again in November. It was reset again for late December but that appearance too was reset upon the granting of a motion filed by defense attorneys. In January of 1970 prosecutor VanValer called to talk to be about the Klan case and about Grand Dragon Chaney. The prosecutor assured me that such delays were standard defense counsel procedure in cases where significant felony penalties were involved. Regarding Chaney the prosecutor asked me if I had ever seen Chaney carrying a weapon.

"Every time I have seen Chaney he's been wearing a gun under has jacket," I noted. "I don't know about carrying weapons in his car, I have never seen the inside of his car and I never want to see the inside of his car either."

VanValer said I may be called to testify about in court Chaney. The following day I received a court order to appear before the Johnson County Grand Jury that was then meeting in secret session. Prosecutor VanValer lead the questioning as I sat in the witness chair before the six-member grand jury. He asked about Grand Dragon Chaney carrying weapons and I related the same information I had given authorities before. One of the Grand Jurors asked me if I had ever been threatened by directly by Chaney.

"No. Not directly. No," I answered.

The whole Grand Jury event for me only lasted about 20 minutes. Since witness testimony was secret I had no idea what else that Grand Jury had been told or who may have also testified. A few days later Chaney was indicted on still another criminal charge of violating the 1935 Firearms Act. He was placed under arrest, posted bond, and was released the same day. On February 24, 1970, for the first time the Klan guard actually entered a plea in Brown County court regarding the charges against him. He plead not guilty to both counts. The trial date was set for May 27, and then a few days prior to that date upon a motion by defense attorneys was reset for September. And in September, now more than a year after the initial armed robbery at the Brown County rally, it was continued until November. On November 20 attorneys for the accused Klan guard appeared in Brown County court seeking a change of venue in the case. That is that criminal charges be transferred from one court to another court in a different location. In this case the different location was Johnson Superior Court. The request was granted.

Thousands of miles away the Federal Bureau of Investigation in San Diego, California had problems with Ku Klux Klan of an entirely different sort. In their office on the morning of January 6, 1971, appearing disheveled and somewhat confused, was a man who went by the name of Thomas Neil

Moore. The man was in fact Gary Thomas Rowe the FBI's Klan informer and now infamous former Klan nightrider. Federal authorities had done almost too well in keeping Rowe from the media, the public and the vengeful United Klans of America. Ironically Rowe, who had reportedly turned down many offers of financial gain from book and movie agents for his life as a Klan double agent (his own book did not do all that well), was now according to a confidential message sent to the FBI's Washington headquarters "experiencing financial difficulties" in his life as Moore. He had no job and seemingly no prospect of finding any immediate employment. Now Rowe wanted to again offer his undercover services to the United States Department of Justice. perhaps as a Federal narcotics agent or as Federal agent aboard flights of major airlines. And while he had no real quarrel with the FBI, he did however have some continuing disagreements with the Justice Department and former Assistant Attorney General John Doar. FBI agents at San Diego listen patiently but did not accept Rowe's new offer.

By the summer of 1971 the FBI still watched developments in the Midwest but from a distance. Beyond the preliminary investigation and limited witness protection, they had been seemingly content with allowing Indiana State Police and local authorities pursue the conviction of the Klan gunman in Indiana. In July, just short of two years after the Klan rally in Brown County, the trial had been delayed for the 12th time. Questioned by a reporter, Johnson County prosecutor VanValer said he had objected to the trial delays. He added further that the aim was to typically handle criminal cases within 60 pages of the arrest or complaint. He allowed however that in general judges tended to recognize difficulties met by attorneys and then showed a willingness to grant continuances in most cases. Asked if he saw any reason to believe, as was asserted the previous week by United States Attorney John Mitchell that the American judicial system, because of such delays, was "drowning in a sea of legalism," the county prosecutor said the problem existed but it was not as bad in Johnson County as in other parts of the United States. That same day Grand Dragon Chaney welcomed and entertained Imperial Wizard Robert Shelton. After a dinner party, Shelton spoke at a Klan rally on the Westside of Indianapolis. This time I wasn't invited.

On the morning of October 8, 1971 the day Napier was to due again to appear in court, I received a visit from one of Chaney's followers, Exalted Cylops Donald Haymaker. Haymaker had telephoned ahead to say he was alone and meant no harm, before actually appearing at the newspaper office. A major reason for the unusual advance phone call, I believe, was to put me as much at ease as possible and to assure there thus would be no real need

Robert M. Reed

for me to call my law enforcement friends. Haymaker had also planned the visit in broad day light with my office typically busy with people.

"Well, you know there is no need to get too upset about all this," a straight-faced Exalted Cyclops told me as we again sat in the Journal conference room.

I looked across the table at him blankly.

Although I didn't know it at the time Haymaker would be giving sworn testimony that very day at the prosecutor's office. It would be ultimately disclosed that in fact that about a half dozen active Klan members and 'shadow' Klan followers had abruptly, - after more than two years of silence, - decided to provide details of the events at the Klan rally which occurred that summer of 1969. Surprisingly, almost shockingly, their accounts not only agreed with each other but agree with mine as well. Yes, this couple was terrorized by the Klan guard. Yes they were held at gunpoint. Yes the camera was taken and the film destroyed. Their multiple versions disagreed with mine on only one essential item. All the Klan forces cooperating at long last with the prosecutor's office maintained that evil guard in the true-life drama was Richardson and not Napier. Security chief Napier, they swore was not even in the vicinity at the time of the assault.

The Klan reasoning was not that hard to figure out. Security chief Napier remained in good standing with the Chaney group. While he had disassociated himself from his role as security chief, he still maintained close ties to the organization. Richardson, on the other hand, was heading a subversive splinter group that was perceived by Chaney's organization as a serious problem for them. Chaney's Klan members had all taken a secret oath to go to the assistance of a fellow Klan member "in any way" in time of danger. Napier was in danger of conviction. Further the secret oath they swore to uphold maintained that "any organization whose existence is an imitation of this order" was to be considered a major offense against their own KKK organization.

Chaney's Klan group saw the opportunity to assist a fellow, if not official, Klan member and at the same time punish a turncoat former member whom they held in contempt as a group. They seized that opportunity.

But the usual talkative Exalted Cyclops made no mention to me that particular morning of what was afoot. Haymaker himself had branched out at this point to also become a member of the National States Rights Party, and a sub-section of which he identified as The Thunderbolt. The National States Rights Party had been the organization of choice also for Alabama's J.B. Stoner, Pennsylvania's Roy Frankhouser, Michigan's Robert Miles, Mississippi's Byron Beckwith, and Mississippi's Thomas Tarrants. (See chapter four). All members of the group had either been charged with or closely associated with violent crimes including murder. All of them had at first belonged to various Klan organizations before finally moving up to the elite ranks of the National States Rights Party.

Haymaker had apparently overlooked any of the NSRP 'alumni', but he did talk in length about Klan organizations and the troubles within their ranks. Although he claimed to not have attended the now pretty much infamous Klan rally in Brown County that Saturday, Haymaker never the less felt he knew a great deal about it from talking with fellow Klan members and from the meetings that followed. As far as the wayward Klan guard was concerned, Haymaker was willing to confirm that Richardson was now heading up the Unified Klan based in Mooresville, but he firmly added, "I am not a part of that at all. No way."

Exalted Cyclops Haymaker also had some other news. In his meanderings that morning, he became the first to raise the strong possibility that some sort of FBI informant or indeed FBI agent was actually present posing as true-believing Klansman the night of the rally. Until then I thought I knew all the gory details of that event. Here was a new twist, be it just Klan talk or something of substance. At least it had my full attention.

"So if the FBI had someone somewhere, why didn't they stop it at the time?," I asked. "How far was it going to go before the FBI agent or informant says enough is enough?"

The Exalted Cyclops just shrugged his shoulders and looked the room, "Ah you know, that's just what I hear. That's the talk. Maybe with your connections, and all, maybe you can find out more."

A few days later I asked detective Bumps about this newly raised FBI agent connection. The FBI, when they interviewed me, had certainly never mentioned it and neither had the prosecutor's office.

"Naw, you don't want to ask about that just now," Bumps responded, just shaking his head.

I decided to let the matter rest for now.

Still the court delays staged by a series of motions filed by defense attorneys continued through the remainder of 1971. Finally in early 1972, Detective Bumps alerted me that the prosecutor's office felt the trial of Klan guard Joe Napier was finally "on." I was skeptical. On Valentine's Day, VanValer called to say the trial would be held on February 14. Unlike prior times, on this occasion the prosecutor went to great lengths to explain his office's preparations on this case and how they were looking forward to jury selection. I would have to testify of course, but he did not want Claudette or I present in the courtroom as the trial opened. We would likely have to take the stand and testify during the second day of the trial. Carefully the prosecutor hinted that the state could indeed have a mystery witness on hand to back up my testimony. VanValer gave no details. Given the extent of time since the whole criminal business started I had no idea of who may or may not be involved in the case. Not only the prosecutor's office, but undoubtedly even the defense attorneys knew more about any witness list than I certainly did.

At home Claudette and I waited for further word. We both expected the late night telephone calls to begin again. They had been frequent early on as any key date in the court proceedings loomed. This time, with this trial date seemingly assured, there were no anonymous telephone calls. On the Monday of the trial I took a rare day off from the office and stayed home with Claudette. At noon the phone rang. Napier had plead guilty to a charge of criminal assault, according to an assistant at the prosecutor's office. In exchange for his guilty plea Napier was given a suspended sentence.

It was, as I told Claudette, at least a conviction. And more importantly for the two of us it was finally over. That afternoon the United Press International moved this item on their newswire as a 'new lead' to their earlier Klan story:

"Franklin, Ind. UPI- A former security guard with the Ku Klux Klan, arrested after a Franklin newsman was robbed at a KKK rally more than two years ago, entered a pleas of guilty to a charge of criminal assault Monday in Johnson Superior Court.

Joe Napier, 45, entered the plea just as the court was preparing to start a jury trial of him on charges of robbery, armed robbery with a deadly weapon and theft from a person. Those charges were dismissed on recommendation of the prosecutor.

Judge Robert Smith sentenced Napier to 180 days at the Indiana State Farm but suspended the term.

The judge also ordered Napier to pay a $1 fine and court costs.

Napier appeared in the court the morning of the trial but entered his plea of guilty before examination of a jury panel began."

The following day I telephoned the prosecutor's office to find out just what had happened behind the scenes to cause them to plea-bargain with the defendant. Prosecutor VanValer had an answer. And was a strange one.

The Sunday evening before the trial as he worked to prepare the case for presentation to a jury the following Monday, VanValer said he received a telephone call from the headquarters of the FBI in Washington, D.C. Presently a caller took the phone and identified himself as an undercover agent. The agent was, he said, present at the fateful KKK rally in Brown County. The reporter's account was true and the crime had taken place. But no, there would be no supporting testimony from the FBI.

And why then, asked VanValer, would they not intercede in this case?

Because, came the reply, the undercover agent was still deeply involved with Klan operations and the greater mission was far more important. True or not that was the account. The prosecutor congratulated me on endurance.

Robert M. Reed

EPILOGUE

> Darkness cannot drive out darkness;
> only light can do that.
> Hate cannot drive out hate;
> only love can do that.
> Martin Luther King Jr.
> Strength To Love, 1963.

A young woman telephoned the office of the Federal Bureau of Investigation in Washington, D.C. on the eve of the nation's 200th anniversary. She was seeking the whereabouts of Gary Thomas Rowe the once famous Ku Klux Klan renegade who, according to media reports, had long since disappeared in the protective arms of federal authorities. She said the man was her own father. In fact—father or not— the former United Klans of America nightrider who had been part of the Klan hit squad which had shot and killed Civil Rights worker Viola Luizzo, had also disappeared from the arms of federal authorities as well. The FBI didn't really know exactly where Rowe was and would not have told the caller if they had indeed known.

What they did not tell the daughter was that the last record of Rowe was his arrest for drunkenness by police in San Diego sometime earlier. Confidential records indicated that while Rowe had apparently made a few obscure telephone calls to the FBI's San Diego office, little else was known of him. Further, said an FBI memo, "it is felt we should not encourage her (the daughter) to request further assistance form the FBI in locating Rowe in the event she is a plant."

Meanwhile back in the Midwest Grand Dragon William Chaney was also having a downturn of luck. Chaney had been able to evade conviction on most of the criminal charges for which he had been arrested in the late 1960s and early 1970s. Skilled and well-paid attorneys either got the charges dropped entirely of won acquittals for their robed client. In 1976 things changed for Chaney. In March of that year during a bitter dispute with his former friend and leader Imperial Wizard Robert Shelton, Chaney was stripped of his rank in the United Klans of America. Chaney would later say of the conflict, "I shook Shelton's hand and told him to kiss Indiana goodbye."

Two months later in May of 1976, Chaney was arrested by law enforcement officers as he apparently fled the scene of a fire bombing in Indianapolis. The target of the bombing had been an outdoor advertising company where Chaney had once worked and served as union president. At the time of his arrest Chaney maintained he was merely driving by the business when his vehicle was stopped by police. However authorities insisted they found a pair of gasoline-soaked gloves on the front seat of Chaney's car.

In the summer of 1976 I had a chance talk very unofficially with James B. Young the United States Attorney for the southern district of Indiana. Attorney Young was a Franklin resident and frequented, as I did, the Franklin Elks Club.

"Wasn't Chaney in touch with you a good deal when the Indiana Klan was being organized?," the US Attorney asked.

"Oh yes. The Grand Dragon got to be quite a visitor for a number of years."

"Has he been in touch with you lately?"

I sensed that perhaps Young wanted more information for his pending federal case. No such luck with me, I explained I had not heard from Chaney in some time.

"Well, you're fortunate," concluded Young, "he's a real bad apple. I think we're gonna send him away for awhile."

Later in federal court Chaney was convicted on all three counts of firebombing. The case was appealed to the Seventh Circuit Court of Appeals in Chicago. The Appeals Court, saying the federal judge may have pressured the jury into the guilty verdicts, upheld the appeal and returned the case for a second trial. With a second trial pending, Chaney was again active in the Ku Klux Klan. During the summer of 1977, at a grouping of various Klan organizations all opposed to Shelton's United Klans of America, Chaney became the compromise candidate to band together the splinter groups. He was selected as the Imperial Wizard for the newly formed Confederation of Ku Klux Klans. Instead of a green Dragon's robe, Chaney was now entitled to wear the Wizard's purple robe. In November of that same year Chaney was found guilty in federal court for the second time on federal fire bombing charges. This time the appeal was rejected and the former Indiana Grand Dragon, and now in 1977 a national Imperial Wizard, was sent to federal prison.

During that same month justice finally found Robert E. Chambliss in connection with the too long "unsolved" 1963 church bombing in Birmingham, Alabama. On November 18, 1977 Chambliss was found guilty in state court on charges of murder and sentenced to life in prison. The former Klansman, once known in police circles as "Dynamite Bob" later died in prison. Upon the arrest of two other Klan members some years later, former Alabama Attorney General William Baxley commented, "the best evidence we had was against Chambliss, so we indicted him first. But they were buddies. They were fellow Klan members."

The telephone at my desk rang and when I answered the caller identified himself as Bill Chaney. My newspaper days were well behind me in the summer 1982 and I was editor of a national publication on antiques and collectibles in a community far removed from my former home in Franklin.

"The newspaper office down there gave me your number," the former Grand Dragon went on, "so I decided to call."

Curious and patent, I waited to hear more.

"Hey," Chaney said, sounding much less robust and confident than he had so many years ago, "would you be interested in doing a story on a World War II hero. Ya, know on a free lance basis?"

Chaney, it seems, had a friend who had just been recognized by the government for bravery decades ago during the war in Europe.

"No," I said, explaining I was pretty well occupied with more specialized writing. I suggested he try contacting the Indianapolis News.

"Well, okay I'll give them a try."

In the next few moments Chaney probably anticipated my parting question.

"Bill, are you still involved in the Klan?"

"Naw," Chaney said finally, "I'm done with that Klan stuff."

Me too, I thought to myself, me too.

Robert M. Reed

BIBLIOGRAPHY

Books

Alexander, Charles C. *The Ku Klux Klan in the Southwest,* Norman, University of Oklahoma Press, 1995.

Allen, Frederick Lewis, *Only Yesterday,* New York, Harper & Brothers, 1931.

Blackstock, Nelson, *Cointelpro,* New York, Pathfinder Book Anchor Foundation, 1988.

Carlson, John Roy, *Under Cover,* New York, American Books-Stratford Press, Inc. 1943.

Chalmers, David, *Hooded Americanism,* New York, Doubleday, 1965.

Churchill, Ward and Wall, Jim Vander, *The Cointelpro Papers,* Boston, South End Press, 1990.

Dees, Morris, *Gathering Storm: America's Mililia Theat,* New York, Harper Collins, 1996.

Gillette, Paul J. and Tillinger, Eugene, *Inside Ku Klux Klan,* New York, Pyramid Books, 1965.

Gitlin, Todd, *The Sixties Years Of Hope, Days Of Rage,* New York, Bantam Books, 1987.

Goldston, Robert, *The Great Depression The United Staes in the Thirties,* Greenwich, Fawcett Publications, Inc. 1968.

Goulden, Joseph C., *The Best Years 1945-1950,* New York, Atheneum, 1976.

Henry, Robert Selph, *The Story of Reconstruction,* New York, Konecky & Konecky, ——.

Nelson, Jack, *Terror In The Night The Klan's Campaign Against the Jews,* New York, Simon & Schuster, 1993.

Perrett, Geoffrey, *Days of Sadness, Years of Triumph,* Baltimore, Penguin Books Inc. 1973.

Rowe, Gary Thomas, Jr. *My Undercover Years With the Ku Klux Klan.* New York, Bantam Books, 1976.

Sims, Patsy. *The Klan.* New York: Stein and Day. 1978.

Sayers, Michael and Kahn, Albert E. *Sabotage! The Secret War Against America.* New York and London, Harper & Brothers, 1942.

Streitmatter, *Mightier Than The Sword,* Boulder, Westview Press, 1997.

Thompson, Jerry, *My Life In The Klan,* New York, G.P. Putnam's Sons, 1982.

Trelease, Allen, *White Terror: The KKK, Conspiracy and Southern Construction,* New York, Harper and Row 1971.

Wade, Wyn Craig, *The Fiery Cross,* New York, Simon & Schuster Inc. 1988.

Wecter, Dixon, *The Age Of The Great Depression 1929-1941,* New York, The MacMillan Company, 1948.

Whitehead, Don. *Attack On Terror: The FBI Against The Ku Klux Klan In Mississippi.* New York: Funk and Wagnall, 1970.

Documents / Reports

Federal Bureau of Investigation, U.S. Department of Justice.

Magazines / Booklets

Alsop, Stewart. "Inside The Ku Klux Klan," *The Saturday Evening Post*, 9 April, 1966.

Flowers, Richmond "Southern Plain Talk About The Ku Klux Klan" *Look,* 3 May, 1966.

Frook, John "Pictorial Summation of a Tragicomic Mistrial," *Life,* 21 May, 1965.

Martin, Harold, and Kenneth Fairly "We Got Nothing To Hide, *The Saturday Evening Post,* 20, January, 1965.

News Wire Services

United Press International
Associated Press

Newspapers

Bloomington Courier Tribune. Bloomington, Indiana.
Brown County Democrat. Nashville, Indiana.
Daily Journal. Franklin, Indiana.
Greenfield Daily Reporter. Greenfield, Indiana.
Greensburg Daily News. Greensburg, Indiana.
Indianapolis News. Indianapolis, Indiana.
Indianapolis Star. Indianapolis, Indiana.
Six County Topics. Bloomington, Indiana.
Spencer Evening World. Spencer, Indiana.

The Courier-Journal. Louisville, Kentucky.
The Franklin Evening Star. Franklin, Indiana.
The Greenwood News. Greenwood, Indiana.
The Republic. Columbus, Indiana.

Robert M. Reed

INDEX

Acher, James D., 86
Ainsworth, Kathy, 59
Alabama, 2, 4, 10, 11, 13, 15, 22, 23, 24, 30, 33, 57, 60, 61, 62, 64, 75, 88, 104, 110
Alabama Knights, 23, 33
American Phalanx, 19
American Protective Association, 6
Andrews, Eliza Frances, Miss, 5
anti-Catholic, 9, 11, 19, 20
anti-Jewish, 9, 18, 19
Associated Press, v, 81, 83, 89, 114
Atlanta, Georgia, 8, 9, 10, 11, 12, 14, 15, 19, 22, 23, 57
Bargersville, Indiana, 27
Bedford, Indiana, 64
Birmingham, Alabama, ix, 17, 30, 31, 110
Black, Hugo, 18
Bloomington, Indiana, 64, 65, 92, 114
Bond, Harvey, 68
Boyd, Alexander, 4
Branham, Wayne, 89
Brown County, 56, 64, 66, 67, 68, 69, 84, 87, 89, 90, 92, 93, 94, 95, 97, 100, 101, 102, 103, 105, 106, 114
Brown County Court, 100, 102
Brown County Democrat, 92, 114
Brown County Jail, 87, 89, 90, 93

Bumps, Richard, v, 44, 45, 46, 81, 83, 86, 89, 90, 93, 94, 98, 99, 101, 105
Bureau of Customs, 24
California, 11, 15, 16, 42, 61, 102
Carlson, 19, 21, 113
Carmel, Indiana, 37
Chambliss, Robert E., 110
Chaney, William, 26, 27, 28, 29, 32, 33, 35, 36, 37, 38, 40, 41, 42, 43, 45, 46, 50, 57, 58, 59, 63, 64, 65, 66, 67, 68, 69, 70, 72, 73, 82, 84, 88, 89, 90, 93, 97, 98, 100, 102, 103, 104, 109, 110, 111
Christian Front, 19
Cincinnati, Ohio, 58
Clansman, 7
Clause, Ed, 4
Colescott, James Arnold, 19, 20, 22
Columbia, South Carolina, 58
Columbus, Indiana, 37, 39, 54, 64, 115
Confederate flag, 28, 36, 62, 67, 68
Confederation of Ku Klux Klans, 110
Courier-Tribune, 92
Daily Journal, 29, 37, 45, 47, 78, 79, 80, 86, 92, 93, 96, 97, 98, 114
Davis, Clarence, 25
Dearborn County, 32, 36

Detroit, Michigan, 20, 21, 29
Dillsboro, 36
Dixon, Thomas, 6, 7, 114
Eads, Terry, 76, 79, 84, 87
Edwards, Eldon, 23
Evans, Doc, 14, 16, 18, 19
Evans, Hiram Wesley, 13
Federal Bureau of
  Investigation, v, ix, 23, 26,
  30, 34, 44, 59, 75, 80, 102,
  109, 114, 121
Florida, 3, 10, 17, 22, 62
Flowers, Richmond, 30, 64,
  75, 76, 114
Forrest, Nathan Bedford Jr., 2,
  4, 14
Franklin College, 39
Franklin Elks Club, 110
Franklin Evening Star, 89, 90,
  115
Franklin Police Department,
  77, 101
Franklin, Indiana, 25, 55, 114,
  115
Frost, J. B., 9
Ft. Pierce, Florida, 62
Furrer, Dale, 29
German-American Bund, 18,
  20
Gillette, Paul, 13, 113
Glover, Gladys, 79, 82
Green County, Alabama, 4
Green, Samuel, 22
Greenfield, Indiana, 27, 37, 43,
  100, 114
Greenwood Police
  Department, 46, 76, 86, 95

Greenwood, Indiana, 26, 27,
  28, 29, 33, 34, 36, 37, 39,
  46, 66, 76, 86, 89, 95, 101,
  115
Gregory, T. W., 6
Griffith, D. W., 7, 8
Hayes, Rutherford, 6
Haymaker, Donald, 37, 103,
  104, 105
Hill, Nat U., 64
Indiana Klans, 68
Indiana State Police, v, 44, 52,
  73, 78, 81, 83, 86, 90, 98,
  101, 103
Indianapolis News, 111, 114
Indianapolis, Indiana, ix, x, 15,
  26, 28, 30, 33, 36, 37, 38,
  43, 45, 46, 57, 59, 67, 76,
  80, 81, 82, 86, 89, 90, 94,
  103, 109, 111, 114
Internal Revenue Service, 22
Iowa, 42
Jackson, Ed, 15
Jackson, Mississippi, 59
Jefferson (KY) Country, 36
Jeffersonville, Indiana, 37, 98
Johnson County, Indiana, v,
  26, 28, 29, 32, 33, 34, 36,
  39, 43, 79, 81, 83, 102, 103
Kennel Club, 38, 39, 40, 41
Kentucky, 22, 27, 36, 43, 115
Klan password, 41
Knights of Kuklos, 1
Knights of the Circle, 1
Knights of the Golden Circle,
  1
Knights of the Ku Klux Klan,
  8, 14, 23, 33

Knights of the White Camellia, 18
Knights of the White Rose, 3
Kokomo, Indiana, 37, 64
Lawrenceburg, Indiana, 27, 32
Liuzzo, Viola, 57, 60
Logsdon, Dan, 78, 79, 80, 81, 92
Louisville, Kentucky, 36, 115
Mariana, Florida, 17
Marion, Indiana, 33, 36
Maryville, Tennessee, 21
Maxwell House, 2
McPherson, Gary, 86, 87, 89
Meridian, Mississippi, 59
Michigan, ix, 3, 13, 18, 20, 21, 25, 29, 37, 42, 59, 60, 63, 68, 77, 100, 104
Michigan City, Indiana, 25
Michigan Klans, 68
Michigan Knights of the Ku Klux Klan, 63
Middletown, 36
Miles, Robert, 59, 104
Minnesota, 42
Monroe County, 63, 64, 100
Montgomery, Alabama, 11, 57, 60
Mooresville, Indiana, 27, 29, 105
Morgan County, 28
Morgantown, Indiana, 65
Muncie, Indiana, 21
Murphy, Matt, 61, 62
Nacirema, 32
National States Rights Party, 58, 59, 104

National Workers League, 19, 21
New Brunswick, New Jersey, 13
New Jersey, 13, 20, 22, 29
New Whiteland, Indiana, 28
New York, 5, 7, 8, 11, 12, 13, 14, 17, 19, 22, 113, 114
New York City, 8, 11, 14, 19
Ohio, ix, 11, 13, 15, 36, 37, 42, 58
Ohio Klansmen, 37
Owen County, 43
Pale Faces, 3
Pennsylvania, 16, 22, 42, 59, 104
Phalanx, 19, 20
Plainfield, Indiana, 37
Pontiac, Michigan, 59
Reed, Harrison, 3
Reed, Judith, 39, 79
Reed, Matthew, 39, 75, 79
Reed, Robert, 1, 2, 81, 89, 90, 121
Richardson, Gary, 96, 100, 104, 105
Richmond, Indiana, 37
Rockford, Illinois, 20, 21
Rogers, Jack, 32
Samaria, Indiana, 66, 84
San Diego, California, 102, 109
Shadoan, Louis, 59
Shelton, Robert Marvin, ix, 23, 24, 27, 29, 30, 31, 32, 33, 34, 35, 36, 42, 43, 57, 58, 59, 60, 61, 62, 69, 103, 109, 110

Shepherd, Clemmet, 75, 77
Silver Shirts, 18, 21
Simmons, William Joseph, 8, 9, 10, 12, 13, 14
Somerset, Kentucky, 27
South Bend, Indiana, 37
South Carolina, 6, 10, 22, 58, 62
Spearsville, Indiana, 65, 66, 87, 94
Spencer, Indiana, 95, 114
Stanley, Jack, 28
Stephenson, David Curtis, 13, 14, 15, 25, 96
Stoner, Jesse Bengamin, 58, 59, 104
Tarrants, Thomas, 59, 104
Tennessee, 1, 2, 11, 21, 22
Terre Haute, Indiana, 19, 37, 57
Texas, 3, 11, 13
Thomas, Eugene, 6, 7, 23, 24, 30, 44, 57, 59, 60, 61, 62, 69, 102, 104, 109, 113
Tillinger, Eugene, 13, 113
Trafalgar, Indiana, 65, 66
Treasury Department, 24
Truman, Harry, 22
Tuscaloosa, Alabama, 23, 30
Tyler, Elizabeth, 9, 10, 12

Unified Klans, 100
union members, 20, 21
United Klans of America, 23, 26, 27, 29, 31, 33, 34, 43, 48, 57, 58, 59, 60, 61, 64, 100, 103, 109, 110
United Press International, v, 53, 80, 81, 89, 106, 114
United States Attorney General T. W. Gregory, 3
United States Secret Service, 24
VanValer, Joe, v, 32, 34, 36, 69, 76, 79, 81, 84, 86, 87, 96, 102, 103, 105, 106
Webb Elementry School, 79
Welsh, Adonijah S., 3
West Virginia, 42
White Brotherhood, 3
White Camellia, 3
Whitecaps, 6
Whiteland, Indiana, 27, 28, 36, 37
Wilkes County, Georgia, 5
Wilson, Woodrow, 7
Wisconsin, 3, 42
Young, Edward, 9
Young, James B., 110
Young, Robert, 84, 89, 94
Zerbe, Harry, 36

ABOUT THE AUTHOR

ROBERT REED is an award-winning journalist who has been honored by numerous organizations including the National Newspaper Association and the Sigma Delta Chi Society of Professional Journalists. His career as a reporter, managing editor and editor spanned nearly twenty-five years.

During the 1960s his extensive reporting on the reemergence of the dreaded Ku Klu Klan lead to a harrowing encounter in a remote Midwestern countryside. Angry KKK guards held both Reed and his wife Claudette at gunpoint during what seemed like an endless night.

Those desperate days, and extensive research including access to thousands of previously classified documents of the Federal Bureau of Investigation form of the core Reed's latest book.

Reed is an accomplished author having written six prior books in the specialized field of antiques and collectibles. Among them are *The Essential Buyer's Guide to Paper Collectibles*, and the current *Vintage Postcards of the Holidays*.

A veteran editor of daily and weekly newspapers, Reed also served as editor of the nationally recognized *Antique Week*. Today he continues to write on antiques and collectibles for numerous publications.

Robert and Claudette make their home in Indiana.

Printed in the United States
6433